Vibrations from Blasting Rock

VIBRATIONS FROM
BLASTING ROCK

L. DON LEET

HARVARD UNIVERSITY PRESS
CAMBRIDGE · MASSACHUSETTS · 1960

Preface

During the thirty years from 1925 to 1955, the quantity of explosives manufactured and used in the United States nearly quadrupled, while the population of the country was increasing about 50 percent. One of the problems accompanying this rapid per capita increase in the use of explosives has been the nature and effect of vibrations generated by their use. This book is an effort by one who has been engaged in research in this field during that period to compile in brief but useful detail the most important factors in this problem. Many of these are not to be found in generally available publications, or have not been published previously.

The material is presented primarily for readers who have had some technical training at some time, but have not necessarily been active in engineering or research in recent years.

L. D. L.

Contents

Tables

Figures

Vibrations from Blasting Rock

Outline of Factors Involved

The process of blasting rock, to facilitate its removal or to obtain crushed stone, involves a series of steps in preparing the blast and a complicated sequence of events during and following detonation of the explosive.

Preparations for a blast begin with drilling holes into the rock for receiving the explosive. The size and depth of these holes as well as their separation from each other and from any free face to which the rock is to be broken have a bearing on the results. The location of the explosive in the holes, and the quantity of rock broken by each pound of explosive (sometimes called the loading ratio or the powder factor), then need to be considered.

Choice of the explosive involves consideration of the properties of explosives and of the rock. Explosives differ in density, in strength, in the rate at which they detonate, in their resistance to water, and in the energy which they apply to breaking rock. Rocks respond to the action of explosives in ways governed by their mineral components and history of formation. They differ widely in the force required to break them, but even more important in determining the effects of blasting are such features as joints, bedding planes, foliation, and variations in their properties brought about by the geological process called weathering.

An explosive is a compound or mixture of compounds that reacts to heat or shock by decomposing rapidly into other compounds, mostly gases. These gases momentarily develop very great pressures as a consequence of their requiring at ordinary pressures much larger volume than that occupied by the explosive. When an explosive buried in rock is detonated, the resulting pressures first shatter by compression a small volume of rock in the immediate vicinity. The pressure front travels away from the explosion through surrounding rock at a speed determined by the properties of the rock. This speed generally is between 10,000 and 20,000 ft/sec. Only recently have the shape and characteristics of this pressure front been determined by accurate instrumental measurements. Very significant practical results have come from these measurements. It has been found that when such a pressure front reaches a rock-air boundary it is reflected back into the rock as a tension front.

The combined effect of pressure and tension at the rock-air boundary is to rupture the rock. This occurs within a few thousandths of a second after detonation. Sometimes, but not always, fragments of the ruptured rock are projected outward. At the same time, expanding gases of the explosion work their way through fractures, churn the pieces, and increase the fragmentation.

Where explosives are distributed among a number of holes, as is usually the case, a technique of detonation has been developed which applies the explosion-generating shock from blasting caps to the explosive in different holes at intervals measured in thousandths of a second. This millisecond or short-period delay in detonations effectively separates the pressure fronts in the rock and the bundles of energy which they deliver to it. Thus the shock fronts break the rock and disturb the unbroken rock not all at once but in a series of closely spaced but independent events. Practical results of this technique have been to improve fragmentation and to reduce appreciably the amount of energy that moves to surrounding territory through the rock as a by-product of the operation in the form of vibrations disturbing to nearby structures.

Of the hemisphere of rock around a blast, only a small fraction of the volume is bounded by a free face close enough to the explosion to be fractured by reflection of the pressure front. In the rest of the rock, the pressure front rapidly decays into elastic waves. Some of these move through the rock, others travel along the surface of the ground. They constitute the vibrations that sometimes shake structures and people.

At the same time, some of the energy escapes into the air and travels as concussion or sound, which is often the only form in which the effects are observed at a distance.

The elastic waves are of several types, each of which travels with a unique velocity that depends on the physical characteristics of the material in which they move. Their speed is greatest in rock, and least in unconsolidated soil and earth, sometimes referred to as overburden. As they travel outward from a blast, these waves become separated progressively by their differences in velocity. Each also dies out as it exhausts its initial energy in moving material along its path. The displacement of the earth's surface as these waves pass is greatest in overburden and least in rock. Special seismographs have been used to study these by-product waves in the ground, particularly in connection with their capacity for damaging buildings or other structures, and incidentally to investigate the characteristics that make them perceptible or annoying to persons.

There have been many investigations of the type and amount of motion due to blast-generated waves necessary to cause damage in buildings. Safe limits have been defined in terms of acceleration, of energy, or of combinations of amplitude and frequency of vibratory motion, and have been widely tested in practice. Vibrations from normal use of different types of buildings have been analyzed for comparison with vibrations in the same buildings from blast-generated waves.

The exact manner in which all these factors are involved when rock is blasted depends upon the type of operation requiring blasting. Rock quarries present one class of conditions. They usually work to a relatively high vertical face and strive for a pile of broken stone at the foot of that face in pieces of a size readily handled by shovels, trucks, and a crusher. On the other hand, they may wish to produce large blocks of the same rock for jetties. They may be working a strong, brittle granite, extensively jointed basalt, variegated limestone, or soft friable sandstone. Each of these involves a special combination of procedures and results. Many trenches in rock are small-scale quarries in a blasting sense, while large road cuts in rock also have many of the blasting problems of a quarry, though they are limited in volume and blasting in them lasts only a short time.

Tunnels present a unique combination of problems. In comparison with quarries or similar operations, tunnels require very small quantities of explosive, and long-period delays of the order of a second or more between detonations, with a free face that is itself buried below the ground surface. The by-product vibrations which affect the neighborhood are correspondingly quite different.

With this quick look at the factors involved in blasting rock, and their relation to one another, let us now consider each separately.

Explosives and Blasting Caps

Most modern blasting explosives date from the introduction of dynamite by Alfred Nobel (1833–1896) in 1867.

Our interest in explosives here is limited to those that have been used in blasting rock. In the continuing search for the best combination of high blasting efficiency and low cost, a problem has been how to evaluate the ability of the explosive to do the required job in different kinds of rock. And it has been found that composition, density, gas ratio, rate of detonation, and energy or strength are characteristics which are important from a technical standpoint. Safety is a universal problem and has always dominated considerations of manufacturers and users alike.

Composition

The most widely used commercial blasting explosives are combinations of carbon, hydrogen, nitrogen, and oxygen so balanced that there is sufficient oxygen to oxidize the carbon and hydrogen to carbon dioxide and steam.

An energy- and gas-producing component such as ammonium nitrate, NH_4NO_3, may be mixed with carbon with a sensitizing compound such as nitroglycerin, $C_3H_5(NO_3)_3$. Pure nitroglycerin is so sensitive that it is dangerous to handle, while pure ammonium nitrate is at the opposite extreme, difficult to detonate, even intentionally. But when these are combined in proper proportions the result is an explosive that has some of the best features of both.

Straight dynamite uses nitroglycerin as the only explosive ingredient. It is seldom used for general blasting, however, because of its relatively high cost, sensitiveness to shock and friction in handling, and very ready inflammability. Replacing some of the nitroglycerin by ammonium nitrate produces a dynamite in which these undesirable features are greatly reduced.

When nitrocotton, produced by treating cotton with nitric acid, is dissolved in nitroglycerin, a jelly is formed that may range from a thick, viscous liquid to a tough, rubbery substance insoluble in water. This is the base for gelatin dynamites. There are also ammonium gelatins in which a portion of the nitroglycerin is replaced by ammonium nitrate.

Compounds that can be made to explode but contain no nitroglycerin and are insensitive with ordinary handling are sometimes referred to as blasting agents, to distinguish them from the more sensitive compounds to which the term high explosive is applied. We will make no special effort to maintain this nicety of terminology here, however, and will generally designate as an explosive anything that explodes, no matter how difficult it is to make it do so.

In the blasting of rock, wide use has been made of explosives that do not contain nitroglycerin and are accordingly characterized by nearly complete safety in handling. Ordinary fertilizer-grade ammonium nitrate in crystallized form (sometimes referred to as prills) is the principle ingredient of some of these, mixed with from 1 to 12 percent of a combustible material such as carbon black, powdered coal, or fuel oil. When fuel oil is used, it may be poured over the ammonium nitrate before loading into blast holes, or it may be poured into the holes after the ammonium nitrate. About 5 to 7 percent by weight of fuel oil gives the best explosive performance.

Density

Technically, the density of an explosive would be the ratio of its mass to its volume, where mass is a number representing the quantity of matter, obtained by dividing weight by acceleration due to gravity. But more convenient ways of expressing this relation are in general use.

Specific gravity is one of these. It is the ratio of the weight of an explosive to the weight of an equal volume of water. The specific gravity of nitroglycerin is 1.6; of 90-percent nitroglycerin gelatin dynamite, 1.55; and of ammonium nitrate with carbon, from 0.8 to 1.0.

Another way of indicating the density of an explosive is to give the number of $1\frac{1}{4} \times 8$-in. cylindrical cartridges, called sticks, packed in a 50-pound case. This ranges from 102 to 175 for straight and ammonium dynamites, and 85 to 120 for gelatin dynamites.

Since specific gravity indicates the concentration of material in an explosive, it is a measure of the compaction of its grains. The shock pressures that produce detonation are communicated through a mass quickly if its grains are close together, but less efficiently if they are loosely packed to give low specific gravity. For this reason, the higher specific gravities are associated with the more explosive compounds.

Gas Ratio

The ratio of the volume at atmospheric pressure of the gas developed by an explosive to the volume of the solid from which it was formed is called the gas ratio of the explosive. Many commerical explosives have a gas ratio of about 8. Ammonium nitrate plus fuel oil has a ratio of about 20.

Some of the actions of explosives in breaking rock are influenced by their gas ratios, but more important in determining total effectiveness is the rate at which the gas is formed.

Rate of Detonation

The chemical changes that take place as an explosive converts from solid to gaseous compounds proceed at different rates in different explosives, or in a given explosive under different conditions of confinement. They may be so slow that the gases escape as they form, and there is simple burning. When they are so fast that they are completed before the gases have time to expand appreciably, the process is called explosion. Detonation occurs when the products of chemical change started by shock or heat set up a pressure jump or shock-wave front, which in turn initiates chemical change in neighboring material. This pressure front moves through the explosive, compressing and heating it to the point of decomposition as it passes. The process, once started, is self-sustaining, and the rate at which detonation moves through it is an important characteristic of an explosive. Velocity is the property of detonation that can be measured most accurately.

Velocities of detonation range from about 4000 ft/sec to about 23,000 ft/sec, for explosives commonly used in blasting rock. Some types of gelatin dynamite detonate at two velocities: about 7000 to 8500 ft/sec when unconfined, and 13,000 to 22,000 ft/sec when confined. On the other hand, even though confined, they may detonate at the lower velocity, or not at all, if subjected to considerable pressures.

Energy

The energy content of an explosive determines the force it can develop and the work it can do. In absolute terms, it is defined in calories per gram or British thermal units (Btu) per pound. In relative terms, it is sometimes called the weight strength, and is expressed arbitrarily as a percentage of the energy of an equal weight of nitroglycerin.

Nitroglycerin or straight dynamites are manufactured with varying fractions of nitroglycerin in their composition. A "60-percent straight dynamite," for example, contains 60 percent of nitroglycerin by weight. It is not three times as strong as 20-percent straight dynamite, however, because there are other energy-producing compounds present. And in going from, say, a 20-percent dynamite to a 60-percent, though the energy obtained from nitroglycerin alone is trebled, the contribution of the other ingredients decreases from 80 to 40 percent, partially counterbalancing the gain from nitroglycerin. As a result, 60-percent straight dynamite is actually about one and a half times as strong as 20-percent.

The effectiveness of an explosive in breaking rock depends on the total energy it releases, the rate at which this energy is released, and the efficiency with which it is transmitted to surrounding rock. These factors are not controlled by any single property of the explosive, of course. On the other hand, total energy content is a very useful characteristic by which to rate explosives relative to each other.

The energy content of explosives has been computed from the composition, density, and heats of formation of the ingredients. [1,2,3]

An important factor that may lead to departures from ideal detonation is a unique characteristic for each explosive, called its *reaction-zone width*. This width is the distance that detonation advances before the products of combustion expand by an appreciable percentage. Ideal detonation requires charges with diameters larger than the reaction-zone width. Effective confinement of the charge reduces the reaction-zone width.

The reaction-zone width of nitroglycerin is less than an inch; of a sensitive initiator like lead azide, N_6Pb, or fulminate of mercury, $C_2N_2HgO_2$, it is a small fraction of an inch; and of ammonium nitrate it is about 9 in.

In Table 1 are listed energy, detonation pressure, and rate of detonation for four explosives. In addition, there is a column showing characteristic impedance, which is defined and discussed in Chapter 4.

Blasting Caps

A very important step in the technology of using explosives was the invention of the *blasting cap* to initiate

[1] F. W. Brown, "Simplified Methods for Computing Performance Parameters of Explosives," *Symposium on Mining Research* (Missouri School of Mines and Metallurgy, Rolla, Missouri, 1957), pp. 123–136.

M. A. Cook, *The Science of High Explosives* (American Chemical Society. Monograph No. 139; Reinhold, New York, 1958).

[3] J. Taylor, *Detonation in Condensed Explosives* (Oxford University Press, New York, 1952).

Table 1. Performance guides for certain explosives [a]

Explosive No.	Specific gravity	Energy (Btu/lb)	Detonation pressure (lb/in.^{2})	Detonation rate (ft/sec)	Characteristic impedance (lb sec/in.^{3})
1	1.6	650	2,939,200	26,250	47
2	1.5	575	2,131,000	22,650	38
3	0.98	450	631,900	13,100	14
4	1.0	436	679,000	13,900	15
	0.8	430	429,000	12,000	10

Explosive 1. Nitroglycerin, $C_3H_5(NO_3)_3$
Explosive 2. 50 percent nitroglycerin, 2.3 percent nitrocotton,
41.5 percent ammonium nitrate, 5.5 percent cellulose,
0.7 percent minor ingredients
Explosive 3. 10 percent nitroglycerin, 80 percent ammonium nitrate,
10 percent cellulose
Explosive 4. 93 percent ammonium nitrate, 7 percent carbon

[a] After F. W. Brown.

detonation. In fact, Alfred Nobel invented the first practicable blasting cap before he completed the experiments that led to the production of dynamite. This first cap was a tin capsule containing fulminate of mercury.

Initiation of detonation was first accomplished by devices that brought flame into contact with the explosive. Modern methods employ electric current and permit high degrees of control through a variety of *electric blasting caps*.

An electric blasting cap is a small cylindrical metal shell, usually of copper. It is commonly $1\frac{1}{2}$ to 2 in. long by about $\frac{1}{4}$ in. in diameter, though delay caps have different lengths.

Figure 1 shows a standard electric blasting cap. It contains two types of explosive compound, a priming charge and a base charge, capped by waterproofing seals. Imbedded in the priming charge is a bridge wire connected to two leg

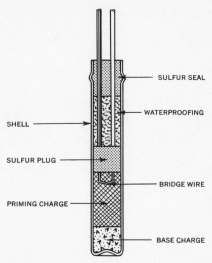

Fig. 1. Electric blasting cap. [From *The Inside Story of Hercules Blasting Caps* (Hercules Powder Company, Wilmington, Delaware, 1957).]

wires that extend outside the cap to carry electric current for firing. Lead azide, N_6Pb, is widely used as a priming charge. Base charges have included such compounds as tetryl, $C_7H_5N_5O_8$, RDX, $C_3H_6N_6O_6$, and PETN, $C_5H_8N_4O_{12}$. When an electric current heats the bridge wire sufficiently, the priming charge detonates. Pressure from this detonates the base charge, and pressure from this, in turn, detonates the explosive in which the cap is placed. These events take place almost instantaneously.

In some types of blasting, it is desirable to apply a firing current to a series of caps all at once, but to have them fire at different times. This is accomplished by the use of delay caps. These contain in addition to the usual elements a delay fuse that is started burning by an ignition agent, and burns for a time proportional to its length before it reaches and fires the priming charge. Figure 2 shows one type of delay cap.

Tables 2 and 3 list delay intervals for various types of

Table 2. Short delay intervals [a]

Delay No.	Approximate firing time (sec)	Delay No.	Approximate firing time (sec)
SP–1	0.025	SP–7	0.205
SP–2	.050	SP–8	.240
SP–3	.075	SP–9	.280
SP–4	.100	SP–10	.320
SP–5	.135	SP–11	.360
SP–6	.170	SP–12	.400

[a] From *Explosives and Blasting Supplies* (Hercules Powder Co., Wilmington, Del., 1953), p. 33.

Table 3. Long delay intervals [a]

Delay No.	Approximate firing time (sec)	Delay No.	Approximate firing time (sec)
1	0.8	9	7.6
2	1.4	10	8.8
3	2.2	11	10.1
4	2.9	12	11.6
5	3.7	13	13.2
6	4.5	14	14.9
7	5.3	15	16.5
8	6.4	16	18.3

[a] From *Explosives and Blasting Supplies* (Hercules Powder Co., Wilmington, Del., 1953), p. 31.

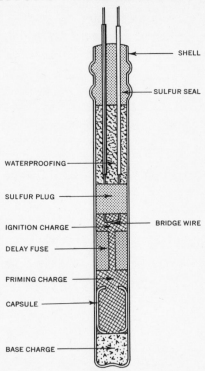

Fig. 2. Short-delay electric blasting cap. [From *The Inside Story of Hercules Blasting Caps* (Hercules Powder Company, Wilmington, Delaware, 1957).]

delay cap. It will be seen from Table 3 that the No. 16 delay cap actually detonates approximately 18.3 sec after electric current has been applied to it.

Primacord

Primacord is the trade name of a detonating fuse with an explosive core of pentaerythritetetranitrate, or PETN,

$C_5H_8N_4O_{12}$. The energy released by exploding PETN is great enough to detonate many explosives if they lie beside it in a borehole. Accordingly, if Primacord is attached to the bottom cartridge in a hole and runs the full length of the hole, it can be used to initiate detonation throughout the entire length of a column of explosives. Primacord is less sensitive than blasting caps to accidental detonation by rough treatment; in fact, there are no instances where it is known to have been responsible for an accidental explosion on blasting operations, even when it was struck by lightning. The Primacord itself is detonated by an electric blasting cap, or equivalent means.

Delay fuse units have been developed for use in long lines of Primacord. These permit delaying the detonation of selected holes relative to others, to achieve the same results as those obtained by the use of short-delay caps.

3

Rocks

Since the breaking of rocks by explosives is the object of
blasting that we are discussing, we need to consider just what
these things are that we call rocks, and their properties that
affect the results of blasting.

Rocks are the commonest of all materials around us.
And even the most casual of observers quickly realizes that
there are many kinds of rock. In terms of earth history, the
first rocks that formed were solidified from a molten mixture,
and all rocks have been derived in some way from these
ancestral types. Rocks formed from a molten mixture are
called igneous rocks. Though they have a common origin,
igneous rocks vary widely in appearance and other properties.
The granite of Bunker Hill Monument and the basalt or
"trap rock" of the Hudson River Palisades are both igneous,
but they are strikingly different in appearance; and granites
and basalts differ significantly among themselves. These
variations result from differences in composition and in the
manner of solidification.

Igneous Rocks

Of the large number of chemical elements that combine to form all matter — at present 102 are known, of which 92 occur in nature — oxygen, silicon, iron, and magnesium make up 90 percent of the materials of rocks, while sodium, aluminum, potassium, and calcium are also present in significant amounts. These most common elements have combined to form nine silicate minerals [1] which dominate the composition of igneous rocks: olivine, augite, hornblende, biotite (black mica), anorthite, albite, orthoclase, muscovite (white mica), and quartz. Igneous rocks are aggregates of interlocking crystals of various combinations of these minerals.

In the first four of the nine common rock-forming minerals — olivine, augite, hornblende, and biotite — the backbone silicon-oxygen tetrahedra are combined with ions of iron and magnesium. These are known collectively as ferromagnesians. They are all very dark or black in color, and have a higher specific gravity than the other rock-forming minerals, mostly over 3.

The five other rock-forming silicate minerals are known as the nonferromagnesians, simply because they do *not* contain iron or magnesium. They are all marked by light colors and relatively low specific gravities, ranging from 2.6 to 3.

The commonest rock-forming minerals of all constitute a nonferromagnesian group known as the feldspars. In the feldspars, aluminum replaces some of the silicon, so they are also called aluminosilicates. The feldspars are subdivided on

---

[1] A silicate mineral is a combination of other elements with Silicon-Oxygen units called tetrahedra. See L. D. Leet and Sheldon Judson, *Physical Geology* (Prentice-Hall, New York, ed. 2, 1958).

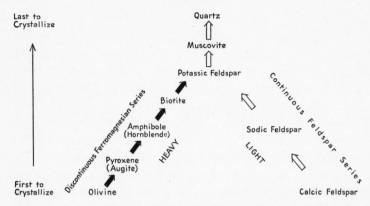

Fig. 3. Bowen's reaction series; the sequence in which minerals crystallize from a magma. [After N. L. Bowen, "The Reaction Principle in Petrogenesis," *J. Geol.*, 30, 177–198 (1922).]

the basis of the manner in which they break when struck a sharp blow, a property called cleavage. Orthoclase is named from the Greek *orthos*, "straight," and *klasis*, "a breaking," because when a piece of orthoclase is broken the two dominant cleavages intersect at a right angle. Plagioclase ("oblique breaking") feldspars are so named because they have cleavage planes that intersect at about 86°.

Quartz, sometimes called silica, is the only rock-forming silicate mineral composed exclusively of silicon and oxygen.

When the materials from which igneous rocks form are still in a molten state, we refer to the mixture as a magma. When magma flows out on the surface, it is called lava. All igneous rocks were formed from the solidification of magma.

The process by which magma solidifies is called crystallization and this proceeds in an orderly manner which influences the types of rock that are formed. Figure 3 shows the sequence in which minerals crystallize from a magma. Actually, a single magma can produce a great variety of rocks as a result of interruptions in the crystallization series. For instance, when crystals of early-forming minerals settle out of a magma they cannot react with it to form new types, as they do if there is no settling. This process is known as fractionation. The rate at which a magma crystallizes influences the extent to which fractionation and mineral changes take place. If a magma cools rapidly, there is no time for crystals to settle or to react with the remaining liquid. But if a magma cools slowly, a high degree of fractionation may take place.

The rate at which a magma crystallizes also influences a physical characteristic of igneous rocks known as texture. In igneous rocks, it applies specifically to the size, shape, and arrangement of the interlocking silicate minerals. When the rate at which a magma cools is relatively slow, crystals large enough to be seen by the unaided eye in hand specimens have time to develop. Rocks composed of such large crystals are called coarse-grained (Fig. 4). Since rapid cooling usually prevents large crystals from forming, the igneous rocks that result have fine-grained textures. Individual crystals are present, but they are so small that they cannot be identified without the aid of a microscope. Occasionally, a magma cools at different rates — slowly at first, then more rapidly. It may start to cool under conditions that permit large crystals to form in the early stages, and then it may move into a new environment where more rapid cooling freezes the large crystals in a groundmass of finer-grained texture (Fig. 5). The resulting rock has a texture which is called porphyritic, and the large crystals are phenocrysts.

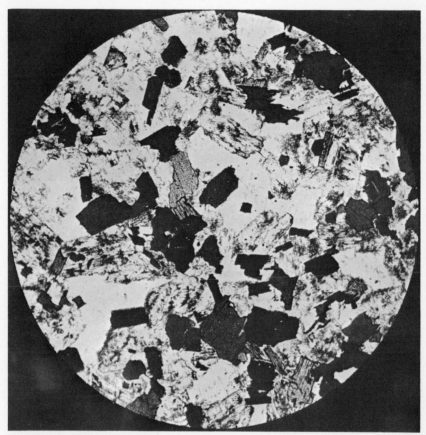

Fig. 4. Thin section of granite. An enlarged photograph of a piece of coarse-grained igneous rock taken through a slice ground to translucent thinness (known as a *thin section*) shows the rock to be compounded of interlocking crystals of different minerals. The diameter of the sample is $\frac{1}{2}$ in.

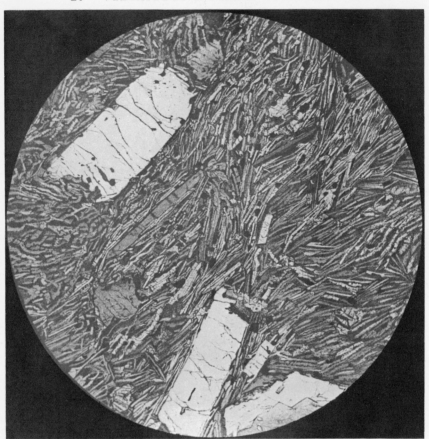

Fig. 5. Thin section of porphyry. The diameter of the sample is $\frac{1}{2}$ in.

A practical classification of igneous rocks is based on texture and composition. This appears in tabular form in Fig. 6, together with a graph that shows the proportions of minerals in each type of igneous rock. The graph gives a better picture of the continuous progression from rock types

IGNEOUS ROCKS
FIELD OR HAND SPECIMEN CLASSIFICATION

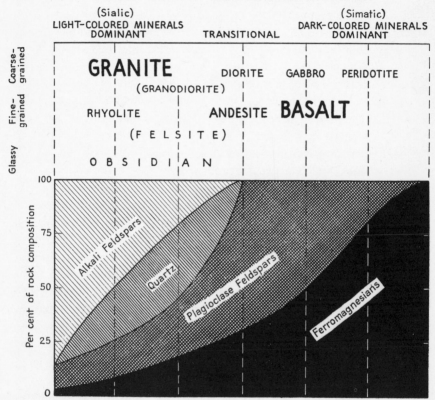

Fig. 6. General composition of igneous rocks, indicated by a line from the name to the composition chart: granite and rhyolite consist of about 50 percent orthoclase (alkali feldspar), 25 percent quartz, and 25 percent divided among plagioclase feldspars and ferromagnesian minerals. Relative importance is stressed by the size of the lettering for rock names: granite is the most important coarse-grained rock, basalt the most important fine-grained rock. [Composition chart modified after Pirsson and Knopf, *Rocks and Rock Minerals* (Wiley, New York, 1926), p. 144.]

in which light-colored minerals predominate to rock types in which dark-colored minerals predominate. The names of the rocks are arbitrarily assigned on the basis of average mineral compositions. Actually, there are many more names in use than are shown in Fig. 6. Sometimes intermediate types are indicated by such names as granodiorite, a composition between that of granite and of diorite.

The igneous rocks on the "light" side of the classification chart are light both in color and in specific gravity. They are sometimes referred to as sialic rocks. The term sial (see-al) was coined from the chemical symbols for Silicon and Aluminum, and is generally used in speaking of the composite of rocks typical of the continental areas of the earth. This composite is dominated by granites and granodiorites and by their allies and derivatives. It has been estimated that granites and granodiorites together comprise 95 percent of all rocks that have solidified from magma trapped within the outer 10 miles of the earth's surface (intrusive rocks).

Granite is a coarse-grained rock. Its mineral composition is 2 parts of orthoclase feldspar, 1 part of quartz, 1 part of plagioclase feldspars, and a small amount of ferromagnesians.

Rocks with the same mineral composition as granite, but with a fine-grained texture rather than a coarse-grained texture, are called rhyolite.

The darker, heavier rocks are sometimes designated collectively as sima (see-ma). This name was coined from *si* for Silicon and *ma* for Magnesium. Of the total volume of rock formed from magma that has poured out onto the earth's surface (extrusive rocks), or solidified in the channels through which such magma reached the surface, it is estimated that 98 percent is basalts and andesites.

A popular synonym for basalt is trap rock, from a Swedish

Fig. 7. A special pattern sometimes found in basalt, known as columnar jointing, consists of breaks in the rock which outline columns that are six-sided in perfect development. This is the Giant's Causeway, near Portrush, Antrim, Northern Ireland, one of the best-known exposures in the world showing this feature. This basalt poured out onto the surface in a series of flows, each 10 to 50 ft thick. (Photo by David M. Owen.)

word meaning "step." This name refers to the tendency of certain basalts to break down into masses that look like giant stairways, as illustrated in Fig. 7.

Basalt is a fine-grained rock. Its mineral composition is 1 part plagioclase feldspars and 1 part ferromagnesians.

Figure 8 shows the contrast in appearance between basalt and granite. Figure 9 shows variations in the appearance of granite brought about by differences in the size of crystals of the individual minerals. The dark ferromagnesian minerals are prominent in this granite. There are others in which ferromagnesians are very inconspicuous, but they are still granites.

Sedimentary Rocks

The original rocks of the globe were all igneous. As surface temperatures dropped to their present levels, water accumulated, and the atmosphere became more as we know it today, the rocks exposed at the surface were subjected to changes by a process called weathering. Alternate freezing and thawing broke pieces off. At the foot of many mountain slopes today you can observe piles of fragments broken from higher cliffs by this process. The water also formed weak acids by taking into solution gases of the atmosphere, and these acids produced chemical changes in some of the rock-forming minerals.

It is weathering that changes rock to soil. And eventually, the products of weathering, such as pieces of rocks or minerals, or in solution in water, are carried by streams to the ocean or other large bodies of water. There they accumulate as sand, gravel, and clay, or are precipitated (sometimes with the aid of shell-forming animals) as new minerals such as calcite, which is a form of the compound calcium carbonate, $CaCO_3$. These are all characterized as sediments.

Fig. 8. Basalt (indicated by hand) cutting through granite. The polished surface of the specimen emphasizes the contrast in texture and color. (Photo by Walter R. Fleischer.)

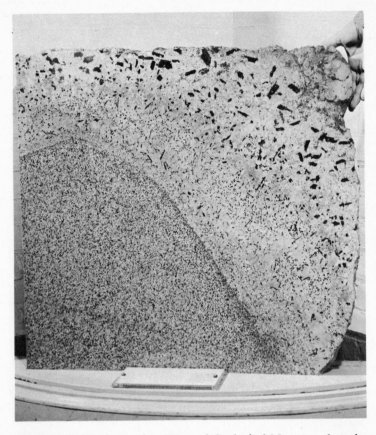

Fig. 9. Variations in granite. (Harvard Geological Museum; photo by Walter R. Fleischer.)

Table 4. Names of rock particles according to size [a]

Particle diameter (mm)	Name
1000.0	
	Boulders
100.0	
	Cobbles
10.0	
	Gravel
1.0	
	Sand
0.1	
	Silt
0.01	
	Clay
0.001	

[a] After E. C. Dapples, *Basic Geology for Science and Engineering* (Wiley New York, 1959), p. 20.

Table 4 gives the names of rock particles arranged according to size. A consolidated gravel is called a conglomerate (Fig. 10).

A rock formed by the cementation of particles of sand size is called sandstone. Clay, which is composed of minerals derived largely from the feldspars, hardens into a sedimen-

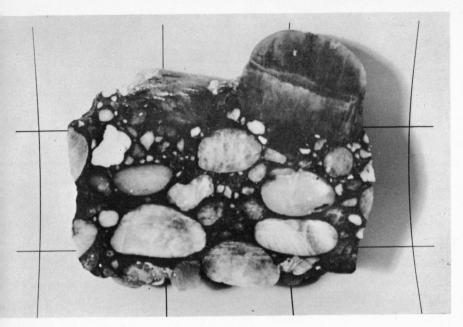

Fig. 10. Conglomerate, a clastic sedimentary rock. The scale is shown by squares, which are 2 in. on a side. (Specimen in Princeton University Museum of Natural History; photo by Willard Starks.)

Fig. 11. A limestone slab marked by the impressions of shellfish which lived on the seabottom where it was forming. The scale is indicated by 2-in. squares on the background. (Specimen in Princeton University Museum of Natural History; photo by Willard Starks.)

tary rock called shale. Rock composed largely of calcium carbonate is called limestone (Fig. 11).

As with igneous rocks, sedimentary rocks have texture: clastic or nonclastic. The term clastic is derived from the Greek for "broken" or "fragmental" and rocks that have been formed from deposits of mineral and rock fragments are said to have clastic texture. Most sedimentary rocks formed by chemical processes have a nonclastic texture, in which mineral grains interlock as they do in igneous rocks. The difference is that the minerals of igneous rocks formed from magma, while those of sedimentary rocks formed from aqueous solutions. Table 5 gives a classification of sedimentary rocks.

Table 5. Classification of sedimentary rocks [a]

Origin	Texture	Particle size or composition	Rock name
Detrital	Clastic	Mixed — granule or larger	Conglomerate
		Sand	Sandstone
		Silt and clay	Shale or mudstone
Chemical		Calcite, $CaCO_3$	Limestone
		Dolomite, $CaMg(CO_3)_2$	Dolomite
Inorganic	Clastic and Nonclastic	Halite, NaCl	Salt
		Gypsum, $CaSO_4 \cdot 2H_2O$	Gypsum
Biochemical		Calcite, $CaCO_3$	Limestone
		Plant remains	Coal

[a] From L. D. Leet and Sheldon Judson, *Physical Geology* (Prentice-Hall, New York, ed. 2, 1958), p. 112.

Sedimentary rocks are often layered, or stratified. Unlike massive igneous rocks, such as granite, most sedimentary rocks are laid down in a series of individual beds, one on top of another. The surface of each bed is essentially parallel to the horizon at the time of deposition, and a cross section exposes a series of layers like those of a giant cake. Stratification is the single most characteristic feature of sedimentary rocks (Fig. 12).

Fig. 12. Alternating beds of sandstone and conglomerate dip inland from the sea cliff at Lobos State Park, near Carmel, California, illustrating the layering or stratification of sedimentary rocks. (Photo by Sheldon Judson.)

The first steps in the sequence leading from igneous to sedimentary rocks occurred over 4 billion years ago. In the great span of time since then many, many changes have occurred. Ocean basins have been squeezed into mountain ranges that were pushed to lofty heights, then worn away and swept over by ocean waters again. Continents have been invaded by the sea and have later risen from it. During such events, both igneous and sedimentary rocks were weathered to form new generations of sedimentary rocks, and in places were subjected to heat, pressures, and chemically active fluids which changed their original characteristics to such an extent that they are classed as metamorphic, or "changed form," rocks.

A very common effect of metamorphism is to rearrange rocks' minerals into parallel or nearly parallel zones of flat or elongated grains. This arrangement gives such rocks a property called foliation; that is, they consist of "leaves," or thin sheets. The usual classification of metamorphic rocks divides them into foliated and unfoliated types.

The foliated rocks have a pronounced tendency, called rock cleavage, to break with greater ease parallel to the layers of mineral grains than in other directions. This often exercises a profound effect on the way such rocks respond to the force of an explosive used to break them.

Some common metamorphic rocks are listed in Table 6.

Although igneous rocks constitute about 95 percent by volume of the outer 10 miles of the earth, about 75 percent of the rocks that we see exposed at the earth's surface are sedimentary rocks, or metamorphic rocks derived from them. Figure 13 shows how the sedimentary rocks limestone and dolomite appear on the face of a quarry after they have been metamorphosed and deformed. The sedimentary veneer thins

Table 6. Common metamorphic rocks [a]

Name	Rock texture	Commonly formed by metamorphism of
	Unfoliated	
Quartzite	granular (breaks through grains)	sandstone
Marble	granular	limestone, dolomite
Hornfels	dense	fine-grained rocks
	Foliated	
Slate	fine-grained	shale, mudstone
Phyllite	fine-grained	shale, mudstone
Schist	fine-grained	shale, mudstone, andesite, basalt
Gneiss	coarse-grained	granite

[a] From L. D. Leet and Sheldon Judson, *Physical Geology* (Prentice-Hall, New York, ed. 1, 1954), p. 342.

Fig. 13. Metamorphosed and deformed limestone beds along the face of a quarry in Lee, Massachusetts. (Photo by L. Don Leet.)

to a feather edge where it laps around the igneous rocks of the Adirondacks and the Rockies. In other places, however, it is thousands of feet thick. In the delta region of the Mississippi River, oil-drilling operations have cut into the crust more than 22,000 feet and have encountered nothing but sedimentary rocks. In the Ganges River basin of India, the thickness of the sedimentary deposits has been estimated at between 45,000 and 60,000 feet.

Shale, sandstone, and limestone make up about 99 percent of all sedimentary rocks. And of these, shale is the most abundant, representing about 46 percent, with sandstone 32 percent and limestone 22 percent.

The Rock Cycle

The relations among igneous, sedimentary, and metamorphic rocks are summarized graphically in the rock-cycle chart of Fig. 14. This traces the various paths that earth materials follow. The outer circle represents the complete uninterrupted cycle. Arrows within the circle represent short cuts that are often taken. An igneous rock, for example, may never be exposed at the surface and converted to sediments by weathering. Instead, it may be subjected to pressure, heat, and chemically active fluids and converted directly into a metamorphic rock. Other interruptions may take place if sediments, or sedimentary rocks, or metamorphic rocks are attacked by weathering before they continue to the next stage in the outer, complete cycle.

Joints

A joint is a break in a rock mass where there has been no relative movement of the blocks of rock on each side of the break. If one side has moved relative to the other, the break

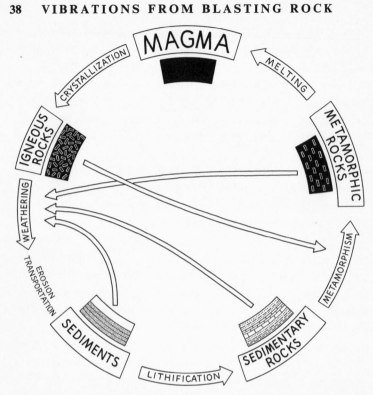

Fig. 14. The rock cycle. Uninterrupted, the cycle will continue completely around the outer margin of the diagram from magma through igneous rocks, sediments, sedimentary rocks, metamorphic rocks, and back again to magma. The cycle may be interrupted, however, at various points along its course, and follow the path of one of the arrows crossing through the interior of the diagram.

is called a fault. Joints occur in all kinds of rock and in every rock exposed at the surface. They are universal, and the most important features that govern the response of rocks to explosives.

The term is said to have originated among British coal

miners who were reminded of the mortar joints that bind bricks or stones together in a masonry waH. But the term is used now even when this resemblance no longer applies.

Joints always occur in sets, never singly. The spacing between joints ranges from just a few inches to a few yards. Usually, the joints in any given set are almost parallel to one another, but the whole set may run in any direction, vertically, horizontally, or at some angle. Most rock masses are traversed by more than one set of joints, often with two sets intersecting at approximately right angles.

Figures 15 and 16 show how joints controlled the breaking of rock blasted for a highway cut.

A pattern of essentially horizontal joints is called *sheeting* (Fig. 17). Here the joints occur fairly close together near the surface, but farther and farther apart the deeper we follow them. After we have traced them a few tens of feet below the surface, they seem to disappear altogether. But even at depth, the rock shows a tendency to break along surfaces parallel to the surfaces of sheeting above. This type of jointing is especially common in masses of granite, and engineers often put it to good use in planning blasting operations. Figure 18 illustrates an example of sheeting in a granite quarry.

Joints exercise so important a control over the pattern of rupture when explosives are used to break rock that if they are steeply inclined (as in Fig. 15), there is serious hazard of slides of rock masses, bounded by joints and loosened by blasting, if the face is nearly parallel to the joints.

Rock Strength

The objective in blasting rock is to break the rock, and the force required to do this is influenced by the strength of the

Fig. 15. When this mass of distorted metamorphic rock with many igneous intrusions was blasted for a road cut, it broke in such a way that a set of nearly parallel major joints stood clearly revealed. They are seen here in shadows, nearly edge-on and inclined slightly from the vertical. They cut indiscriminately through the twisted metamorphic rock and massive igneous rock. Highway 2, near West Acton, Massachusetts. (Photo by L. Don Leet.)

Fig. 16. Joint planes blocked out pieces of massive sialic rock by providing surfaces of easy breakage when this rock was blasted for road construction. (Photo by L. Don Leet.)

Fig. 17. Sheeting in granite accentuated by weathering. (Photo from Gardner Collection, Harvard University.)

Fig. 18. Sheeting in granite revealed by quarrying. (Photo by Sheldon Judson.)

Table 7. Strength of rocks [a]

Rock	Modulus of rupture (lb/in.^{2})	Compressive strength (lb/in.^{2})	Tensile breaking strain [b] (10^{-6}in./in.)
Granite	2700–3900	28,400–39,500	380
Basalt	2500–6600	26,600–52,000	
Sandstone	400–3600	6,100–34,100	560
Shale	2200–5000	15,600–45,800	
Limestone	400–3800	9,700–37,600	310
Marble	1700–3300	18,000–33,000	
Gneiss	1200–3100	22,200–36,400	
Amphibolite [c]	4200–7400	30,400–74,900	
Greenschist [d]	3200–6700	17,700–45,500	

[a] S. L. Windes, *Physical Properties of Mine Rock* (U.S. Bureau of Mines, Report of Investigations 4459; Government Printing Office, Washington, 1949).

[b] W. I. Duvall and T. C. Atchison, *Rock Breakage by Explosives* (U.S. Bureau of Mines, Report of Investigations 5356; Government Printing Office, Washington, 1957).

[c] Amphibolite is a faintly foliated metamorphic rock composed mainly of hornblende and plagioclase feldspars, developed during the metamorphism of simatic rocks.

[d] Greenschist is a schist characterized by green color imparted by the mineral chlorite. It is formed by the metamorphism of simatic rocks.

Table 8. Longitudinal-wave speeds and characteristic impedances for certain rocks

Rock	Longitudinal-wave speed (ft/sec)	Characteristic impedance (lb sec/in.^{3})
Granite	18,200	54
Marlstone [a]	11,500	27
Sandstone	10,600	26
Chalk [b]	9,100	22
Shale	6,400	15

[a] Marlstone is a hardened mixture of clay materials and calcium carbonate, normally containing 25 to 75 percent of clay. It is a type of limestone.

[b] Chalk is a very soft limestone.

rock. But this is not as simple as it sounds, because rocks have different kinds of strength. A piece of granite subjected to pressure on all sides may not break until this pressure reaches 35,000 lb/in.[2] (*compressive strength*), while a rod of it can be pulled apart by a force of 1000 lb/in.[2] (*tensile strength*), or if it is supported on both ends and bent in the middle, it may break under 3000 lb/in.[2] (*modulus of rupture*). We will see later in the discussion of mechanism of rupture by blasting forces that compressive and tensile strengths may be of particular interest. It happens, however, that because of standardization of test procedures[2] there are more data on modulus of rupture than on tensile strength. Since modulus of rupture roughly parallels tensile strength for different rocks (it is around three times as great), it is a helpful guide to differences among rocks in their response to forces applied by blasting.

Table 7 lists some strength criteria for representative igneous, sedimentary, and metamorphic rocks.

There are two other characteristics of rocks that are important in determining their reaction to vibrations from blasting. These are elasticity, which is measured by the velocity with which longitudinal waves traverse the rock (see Chapter 5), and characteristic impedance, which is defined and discussed in Chapter 4. To keep specific rock properties together for convenience, Table 8 lists some values of longitudinal wave speeds and characteristic impedance.

[2] Leonard Obert, S. L. Windes, and W. I. Duvall, *Standardized Tests for Determining the Physical Properties of Mine Rock* (U.S. Bureau of Mines, Report of Investigations 3891; Government Printing Office, Washington, 1946).

4

Rupture of Rock by Blasting

If an explosive is placed in a hole drilled in rock and is then detonated, the first result is development of high pressures from the gases that form. Table 1 gives some of these pressures. Those listed in this table cover the range of pressures from explosives commonly used for blasting rock, and all exceed the greatest strength of all rocks (see Table 7). As a result, rock immediately around the explosive is crushed (Fig. 19). The pressures fall very quickly, however, to values below the compressive strength of the rock. Then the crushing stops and the remaining energy moves into unbroken rock as a wave of pressure, sometimes called the *shock front*, traveling at approximately the speed of sound in the same rock but not breaking it.

Within a few feet of the crushed zone, if the shock front reaches a free face, that is, a surface where rock stops and air begins, the wave of pressure is reflected back into the rock as a wave of tension. Momentarily, then, a few inches back of the free face, rock is being pushed outward by trailing parts of the pressure wave and at the same time pulled outward by the reflected tension wave. If the combination

Fig. 19. Quarry face after a blast of 27 holes. The light-colored vertical streaks on the face are caused by the higher reflectivity of zones of rock crushed for a few inches behind each column of explosive.

of these two gives a total strain great enough, the rock breaks off. The onrushing remainder of the pressure wave then finds a new free face to reflect it as a tension wave, and the process may repeat itself several times. The exact number of such repetitions, in fact, can be predicted from data on the length of the pressure wave, combined with the tensile strength of the rock.

If the charge is large enough, crushing of rock immediately around the explosive and rupture by reflection of the shock front from a free face are followed by pressures of the expanding bubble of hot gases which push the remaining rock toward the free face as they churn and break it in escaping to the air.

Crater Tests

A great deal about the mechanism of breaking rock by a reflected shock front was learned from studying craters produced by charges buried in rock.[1]

[1] W. I. Duvall and T. C. Atchison, *Rock Breakage By Explosives* (U.S. Bureau of Mines, Report of Investigations 5356; Government Printing Office, Washington, 1957). This publication contains an extensive bibliography.

When a crater test was conducted, a charge of explosive was placed in a hole drilled into rock. Granular material, called stemming, was used to fill the rest of the hole. Usually the hole was vertical. The explosive was then detonated, broken rock was removed, and the dimensions of the crater were determined. Figure 20 illustrates some of the terms used in reporting the results.

Some of the results of crater tests are illustrated in Figs. 21, 22, 23, and 24, for granite, limestone, and sandstone.

A striking feature of these results is the relation between depth of charge and depth of the resulting crater. A charge at shallow depth produced a small crater that bottomed at the charge depth. Placing the same charge deeper produced

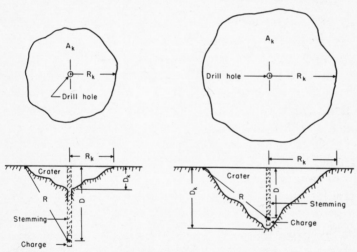

Fig. 20. Crater terminology: D, depth of center of gravity of charge of explosive; A_k, surface area of crater; R_k, surface radius of crater, with $\pi R_k^2 = A_k$; R, radius of rupture $= (D^2 + R_k^2)^{\frac{1}{2}}$, or the average distance from the center of the charge to the periphery of the crater at the surface; D_k, depth of crater.

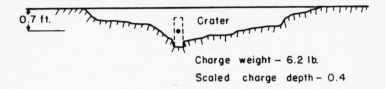

0.7 ft.

Crater

Charge weight – 6.2 lb.

Scaled   charge   depth – 0.4

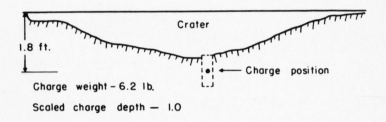

1.8 ft.

Crater

Charge   position

Charge weight – 6.2 lb.

Scaled charge   depth — 1.0

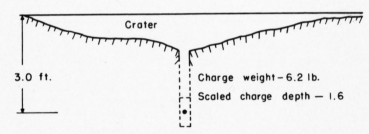

Crater

3.0 ft.

Charge   weight – 6.2 lb.

Scaled   charge   depth — 1.6

Fig. 21. Crater sections in granite. The scaled charge depth is $D/\bar{r}$, where $\bar{r}$ is the depth in feet divided by the cube root of the explosive charge weight in pounds.

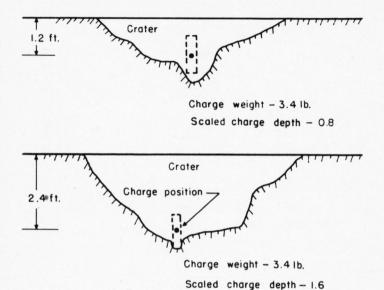

Charge weight – 3.4 lb.
Scaled charge depth – 0.8

Charge weight – 3.4 lb.
Scaled charge depth – 1.6

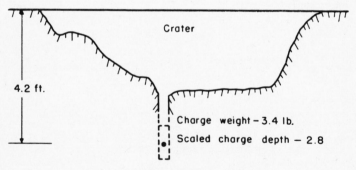

Fig. 22. Crater sections in marlstone.

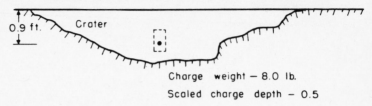

Charge weight — 8.0 lb.
Scaled charge depth — 0.5

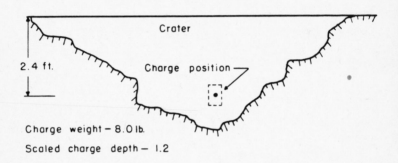

Charge weight — 8.0 lb.
Scaled charge depth — 1.2

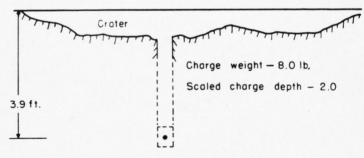

Charge weight — 8.0 lb,
Scaled charge depth — 2.0

Fig. 23. Crater sections in sandstone.

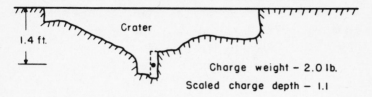

1.4 ft.

Crater

Charge weight – 2.0 lb.
Scaled charge depth – 1.1

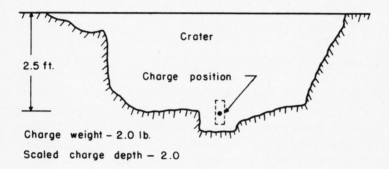

2.5 ft.

Crater

Charge position

Charge weight – 2.0 lb.
Scaled charge depth – 2.0

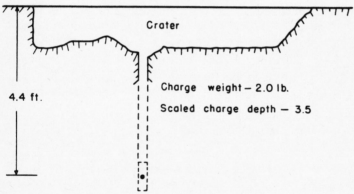

4.4 ft.

Crater

Charge weight – 2.0 lb.
Scaled charge depth – 3.5

Fig. 24. Crater sections in marlstone.

a larger crater at first; then, as depth increased still more, the crater radius remained about the same but the crater depth was significantly less than the charge depth. Finally (not illustrated in the figures), charge depths were reached in all rocks where no crater was produced.

There was evidence in some of the crater tests that the breakage of rock to form the craters was the result of force transmitted through rock that itself remained unbroken in the transmission process. In those tests, however, there was still a connection from the charge location to the ultimate crater by way of the drill hole used for placing the charge. So presumably gases could have traveled up the hole and participated in crater formation. To investigate this possibility, the Bureau of Mines conducted a special series of tests in a limestone in which the explosive charge was placed by the use of horizontal holes, and there was no connection by drill hole or other opening from the charge to the surface.

The results of these tests are illustrated in Figs. 25 and 26. The horizontal holes were sand-stemmed, and long enough that gases did not escape through them. Gases also failed to reach the surface. They cooled, contracted, and moved into voids and fissures within the rock. So all crater formation was accomplished by the reflected shock front, and solid unbroken rock remained between the crater and the explosive, while escaping gases did not participate at all in crater formation. When charge depth was so great that no crater formed, there was still cracking in the shape of a crater in some cases, outlining a *potential crater zone*. This potential crater zone has an important bearing on effects at the surface in some types of blasting, as will be discussed later.

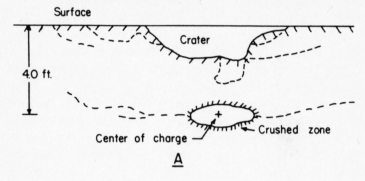

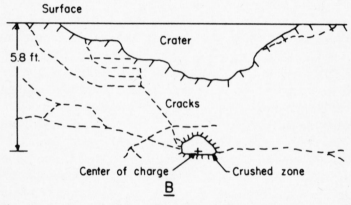

Fig. 25. Sections of crater tests where charge was loaded through horizontal holes in chalk: *A*, 1.5-lb charge weight, 3.5 scaled charge depth; *B*, 3.0-lb. charge weight, 4.0 scaled charge depth.

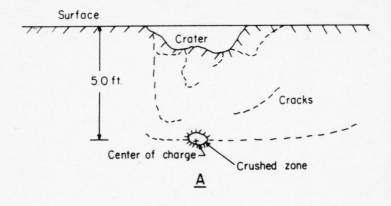

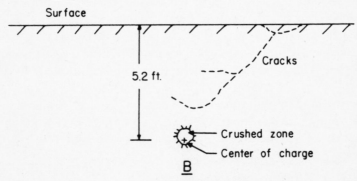

Fig. 26. Sections of crater tests where charge was loaded through horizontal holes in chalk: *A*, 0.8-lb charge weight, 5.4 scaled charge depth; *B*, 0.38-lb charge weight, 7.0 scaled charge depth.

Laboratory Tests

The rupture of rock by reflected waves has also been demonstrated in laboratory tests.[2] In these, an explosive detonated against one end of a 20- to 30-cm prism of rock caused the rock to split off from the opposite end by reflected-tension rupture into three or more slabs.

Strain Waves in Rock

As energy from an explosion moves into unbroken rock outside the zone of crushing, it causes a sudden rise in pressure as it passes. This displaces the rock in its path. The manner in which rock is thus displaced by the shock front has been investigated theoretically and by experiment.[1, 3-6]

Such investigations have considered rock displacement, velocity, acceleration, and strain as functions of time. Between the zone of crushing and a free face where rupture by reflection is produced, rock strain is particularly significant. It has been measured in microinches per inch, that is, 10^{-6} in./in.

It has been found that within the first few feet strain rises abruptly to a maximum, then takes a longer time to decrease to zero; but the strain is not oscillatory in this zone. As

[2] Kumao Hino, "Fragmentation of Rock Through Blasting," *Industrial Explosives Soc. Japan 17*, 2–11 (1956).

[3] J. A. Sharpe, "The Production of Elastic Waves By Explosion Pressures: I. Theory and Empirical Field Observations," *Geophysics 7*, 144–154 (1942).

[4] Leonard Obert and W. I. Duvall, *Generation and Propagation of Strain Waves in Rock. Part I* (U.S. Bureau of Mines, Report of Investigations 4683; Government Printing Office, Washington, 1950).

[5] W. I. Duvall, "Strain-Wave Shapes in Rock Near Explosions," *Geophysics 18*, 310–323 (1953).

[6] W. I. Duvall and Benjamin Petkof, *Spherical Propagation of Explosion-Generated Strain Pulses in Rock* (U.S. Bureau of Mines, Report of Investigations 5483; Government Printing Office, 1959).

distance increases, changes in strain tend to become oscilla-tory, with at least one complete cycle. Distances from an explosion are "short" or "long" in terms of the radius a of the crushed zone or explosion cavity. This, in turn, is deter-mined by the amount of explosive and by the characteristics of the rock. Figure 27 shows the computed variation of strain with time, for an arbitrarily assumed initial pressure varia-tion, at distances of $2a$, $5a$, and infinity. It illustrates the transition from nonoscillatory to oscillatory character.

Propagation of Strain

Duvall and Petkof [6] reported that the peak strain pro-duced in rock by the detonation of a concentrated charge of explosive is given by the equation

$$\epsilon = \frac{K_w}{\lambda} e^{-\alpha\lambda},$$

where ϵ is the peak strain, K_w is the propagation constant, $\lambda = R/W^{\frac{1}{3}}$ is the scaled distance from the explosive to the point in question, R (ft) is this absolute distance, W (lb) is the weight of the explosive, α is the absorption constant, and e is the base of natural logarithms.

They found, also, that K_w correlated with the detonation pressure of the explosive P:

$$K_w = kP,$$

so that

$$\epsilon = k\frac{P}{\lambda} e^{-\alpha\lambda},$$

where k and α are constants for a given rock; α does not differ significantly from 0.03 for many common types of rock. If V_p is the velocity of compressional waves in a rock

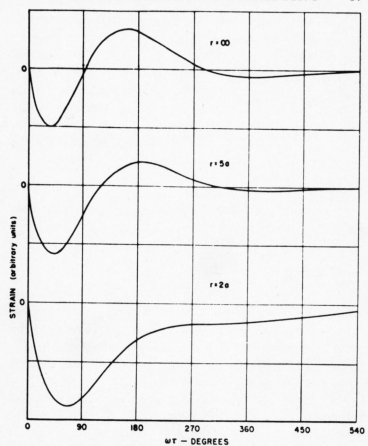

Fig. 27. Shape of strain-wave pulses for an arbitrarily assumed pressure, at distance of 2*a*, 5*a*, and infinity, where *a* is the radius of the crushed zone or explosion cavity. After Duvall.

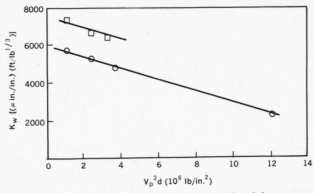

Fig. 28. Relation between the elastic constant $V_p^2 d$ and the propagation constant K_w for rock: *circles*, semigelatin 2 (detonation pressure, 0.95×10^6 lb/in.^{2}); *squares*, 60-percent ammonia gelatin (detonation pressure, 1.29×10^6 lb/in.^{2}). (After Duvall and Petkoff.)

it and d is its density, the product $V_p^2 d$ is the elastic constant of the rock. The relation between K_w and $V_p^2 d$ is shown in Fig. 28, which completes the information necessary to compute peak strain when explosive and rock properties are known.

Strain Measurements

Figure 29 illustrates the terminology used in describing strain record measurements, and Figs. 30, 31, 32, and 33 show some typical strain records obtained by the Bureau of Mines.

Duvall and Atchison[1] found that the ratio of fall strain e_f to the strain that breaks a given rock governs the number of slabs broken off by reflection of the strain pulse. The number of slabs is the first whole number less than that ratio.

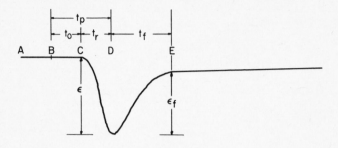

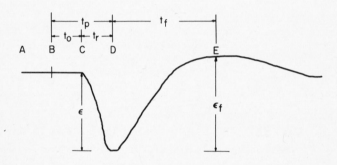

A = Start of trace

B = Detonation of charge

C = Start of strain pulse

D = Peak of compressive strain

E = End of fall strain

t_0 = Arrival time for start of pulse

t_r = Rise time

t_f = Fall time

t_p = Arrival time for peak strain

ϵ = Peak compressive strain

ϵ_f = Fall strain

Fig. 29. Terminology for strain records.

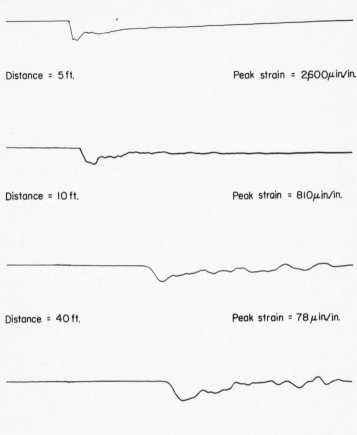

Distance = 5 ft.   Peak strain = 2,600 μin/in.

Distance = 10 ft.   Peak strain = 810 μin/in.

Distance = 40 ft.   Peak strain = 78 μin/in.

Distance = 50 ft.   Peak strain = 50 μin/in.

24 lb. semigelatin, type A   Time scale - |⟵⟶| = 1 millisecond

Fig. 30. Strain records of U.S. Bureau of Mines in marlstone.

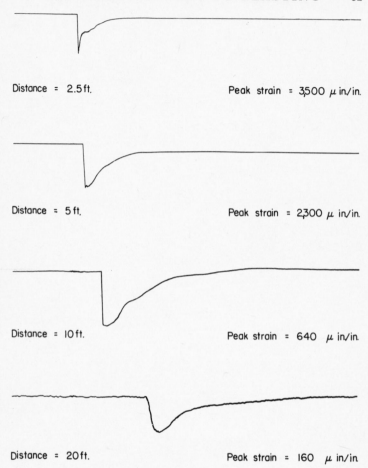

Distance = 2.5 ft.   Peak strain = 3,500 μ in/in.

Distance = 5 ft.   Peak strain = 2,300 μ in/in.

Distance = 10 ft.   Peak strain = 640 μ in/in.

Distance = 20 ft.   Peak strain = 160 μ in/in.

8 lb. ammonia dynamite   Time scale - |←——→| = 1 millisecond

Fig. 31. Strain records of U.S. Bureau of Mines in sandstone.

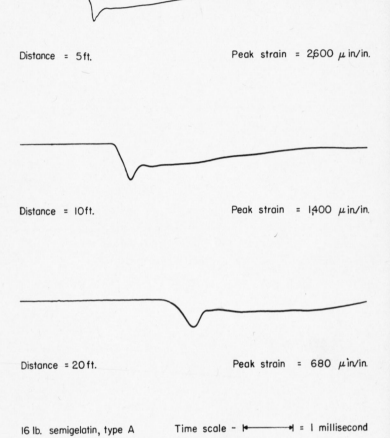

Distance = 5 ft.   Peak strain = 2,600 μ in./in.

Distance = 10 ft.   Peak strain = 1,400 μ in./in.

Distance = 20 ft.   Peak strain = 680 μ in./in.

16 lb. semigelatin, type A   Time scale — |——————| = 1 millisecond

Fig. 32. Strain records of U.S. Bureau of Mines in chalk.

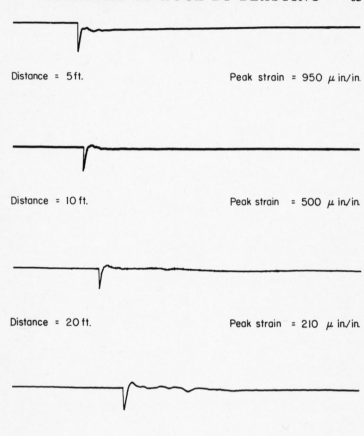

Distance = 5 ft.   Peak strain = 950 μ in./in.

Distance = 10 ft.   Peak strain = 500 μ in./in.

Distance = 20 ft.   Peak strain = 210 μ in./in.

Distance = 40 ft.   Peak strain = 58 μ in./in.

3.9 lb. gelatin, type B   Time scale – |←——→| = 1 millisecond

Fig. 33. Strain records of U.S. Bureau of Mines in granite.

In crater formation, these same authors found that the depth of a crater is approximately equal to half of the fall length of the strain pulse, provided this is less than the charge depth and the fall strain is several times larger than the breaking strain of the rock. The fall length of a strain pulse is the fall time t_f multiplied by the velocity with which the strain pulse travels in the rock. If the fall length is greater than the charge depth, rock breaks only from the free surface back to the crushed zone around the charge.

Transfer of Energy from Explosive to Rock

In the blasting of rock, breakage is directly related to the amount of energy transferred from the explosive to the rock and the efficiency with which this energy is transmitted through the rock.

U.S. Bureau of Mines investigators [7] found that, of the total energy computed for several test explosives, from 10 to 20 percent was transferred to a granite in which the explosives were detonated. They pointed out, moreover, that within the range of their experiments the amount of energy transferred to a given rock was a linear function of the product of density and rate of detonation, which they called the *characteristic impedance* of the explosive. They also defined a characteristic impedance for rock: density times velocity of longitudinal waves in the rock. The conclusion was that "explosives that had the larger characteristic impedances, or impedances more nearly matching the characteristic impedance of the rock, transferred more energy to the rock."

In this connection, the method of packing explosives into

[7] D. E. Fogelson, W. I. Duvall, and T. C. Atchison, *Strain Energy in Explosion-Generated Strain Pulses* (U.S. Bureau of Mines, Report of Investigations 5514; Government Printing Office, Washington, 1959), p. 15.

boreholes becomes a factor, since the impedance of both rock and explosives is of the order of 10,000 times that of air. This very large contrast in impedances causes serious losses in transferring energy from explosive to air and from air to rock.

The Expanding Gases

In most commercial blasting, the rupture of rock by reflected strain pulses is supplemented by work done by the expanding gases of an explosion. These supply the energy which moves the entire rock mass, or burden, that is broken from a face and deposited in fragments at its base.

Noren [8] studied burden movement under controlled conditions at a $2 \times 7 \times 6$-ft cut on a bench in an experimental tunnel. He found that for a given quantity of explosive massive movement of the burden began after an interval which was proportional to the thickness of the burden and several times greater than the time required for the shock wave to reach the face and produce cracking by reflection. The velocity with which the burden moved out was inversely proportional to the square root of the rock weight.

Effect of Rock Features

The general principles of rock rupture by blasting have been established primarily on the basis of investigations carried out on small volumes of nearly uniform rock masses. Rupture by reflected tension waves, for example, was studied in small-scale crater tests and in laboratory tests such as we have reviewed above, and massive movements of burden

[8] C. H. Noren, "Blasting Experiments in Granite Rock," *Quart. Colo. School Mines 51*, 212–225 (1956).

produced by expanding gases were measured on small volumes in shallow bench blasting.

These two mechanisms accomplish the rupture of rock, but cannot be used to explain the details of breaking in most actual commercial operations, because such details are governed to a high degree by features of the rock itself.

Joints, whether open and prominent or so tightly closed as to be invisible, are surfaces along which rock is actually broken before any blasting takes place or has tensile, bending, or shear strengths either negligible or at least far below those of uniform joint-free specimens used in laboratory tests. As a result, these are the surfaces of easiest rupture regardless of the mechanism, and they control the shapes and to some degree the sizes of the pieces into which rock breaks. Joints are present in every rock type. Their importance among factors controlling rock rupture can hardly be over-estimated.

Bedding planes in sedimentary rocks and directions of foliation in metamorphic rocks also represent regions of special weakness.

The composition and geological history of rock are controlling factors in rock rupture and must be fully considered in any program for blasting rock.

5

The Elastic-Wave Pattern

We have seen how the energy released by detonation of an explosive first crushes rock in the immediate vicinity, then moves through the next few feet as a shock front or strain pulse. This quickly becomes an oscillatory wave in which the particles along the path of travel move in orbits that repeat cyclically. The simplest two-dimensional illustration of such an oscillation is a wave shape with a crest and a trough. From there on, the energy produces movements in rock or other materials that are within their elastic limit. In other words, the materials recover completely from any displacements to which they are subjected and after the energy has passed return to their original shape and volume. The waves in this region are accordingly called *elastic waves*.

Elastic Waves in the Ground

The initial shock front outside the zone of rock shattering applies force to the rock through which it moves, in such a way as to compress it or reduce its volume. In the elastic zone, this causes wave motion similar to that by which sound is transmitted through a fluid or a solid. Particles in the path

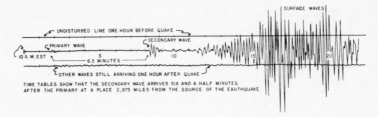

Fig. 34. An earthquake record which shows the division into wave groups that led to the original use of the terms primary waves and secondary waves.

of such waves move back and forth along the line of advance of the waves, and the waves are called *longitudinal, compressional, push-pull,* or *primary waves.* The term primary comes from the fact that this wave type travels faster than any other elastic waves in a given material and is the first to arrive at distant points (Fig. 34). From the designation primary, the symbol *P* has been taken to represent these waves.

Where the initial pressure pulse, or the *P*-wave into which it degenerates, strikes a free surface or a change of material at any angle other than head-on, there are complicated displacements which shear or change the shape of the transmitting material in addition to compressing it. This gives rise to a new wave type, called the *shear, shake,* or *secondary wave* (symbol *S*). The term secondary came into use in the early days of studying waves from earthquakes, when the second of three prominent groups of waves was identified as trains of shear waves.

P-waves can travel in a solid, liquid, or gas because these forms of matter resist compression or volume change. *S*-waves can travel only in a solid, because their existence depends on the existence of a shear modulus, or the ability

of a transmitting material to resist changes in shape. Both *P*-
and *S*-waves travel into and through the body of the materials
which transmit them, and for that reason are sometimes
classed together as *body waves*.

In contrast to body waves in the ground, there are others
which travel only on a free surface where the solid elastic
materials transmitting them are bounded by air or water.
These are known collectively as elastic *surface waves*. If a
picture of the ground surface could be taken as some of these
pass (it cannot because even from the largest earthquakes
such waves are not high enough to show up), it would reveal
the surface wrinkled into a turbulent series of crests and
troughs not greatly different from the surface of a body of
water ruffled by wind or other disturbances. Unlike waves
on water, however, surface waves in the ground are of several
types. Each is defined by the motion through which a particle
in its path goes as the wave passes. If we define directions in
terms of the way the wave is traveling, we can say that a push
is a forward displacement along the line of the wave's advance
and a pull is a displacement in the opposite direction. Then
left and right would be displacements at right angles to a
push, as viewed by an observer facing in the direction of the
wave's advance. Up and down are self-explanatory.

One type of surface wave causes a particle in its path to
move in an elliptical orbit, in the sense push–up–pull–down,
and so on (Fig. 35). This wave was first predicted mathematically by Lord Rayleigh [1] and is known as the *Rayleigh
wave*, with the symbol *R*. Such waves were identified on

---

[1] John William Strutt, Baron Rayleigh, "On Waves Propagated Along the
Plane Surface of an Elastic Solid," *Proc. London Math. Soc. 17*, 4–11 (1885);
Scientific Papers (Cambridge University Press, Cambridge, 1900), p. 447.

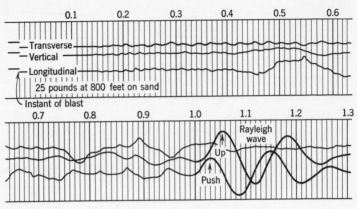

Fig. 35. Record of a Rayleigh wave.

earthquake records in 1931 [2] and later among waves generated by dynamite blasts [3] and by the first A-bomb.[4]

Another type of elastic surface wave is one in which particles of the transmitting material vibrate transverse to the direction of the wave's advance, *with no vertical displacements*. This is called a Q-wave, from the German *querwellen*, or Love wave (but not represented by the symbol L) after the British scientist A. E. H. Love, who explained it mathematically.[5]

A third type of elastic surface wave that has been identified

[2] L. D. Leet, "Empirical Investigation of Surface Waves Generated by Distant Earthquakes," *Publications of the Dominion Observatory*, vol. 7, "*Seismology*," No. 6 (Ottawa, 1931).

[3] L. D. Leet, "Ground Vibrations Near Dynamite Blasts," *Bull. Seis. Soc. Am. 29*, 487–496 (1939).

[4] L. D. Leet, "Earth Motion From the Atomic Bomb Test," *Am. Scientist 34*, 198–211 (1946).

[5] A. E. H. Love, *Some Problems of Geodynamics* (Cambridge University Press, Cambridge, 1911), pp. 144–178.

moves a particle in its path along a diagonal line in the sense push–left–up then pull–right–down, or push–right–up then pull–left–down. This was first observed in 1939 from records of dynamite blasts [3] and later observed in ground motion at the first atomic-bomb test. [4] It is called the coupled wave, with symbol C, because it suggests combined motion of a P-type and an S-type.

A fourth type of elastic surface wave caused the greatest ground motion at the test of the first atomic bomb. [4] It moves a particle in its path around an elliptical orbit as does the Rayleigh wave, but in the opposite sense: push–down–pull–up. Because this is the general sense of motion in the path of a wave on water, this elastic surface wave was named the hydrodynamic or H-wave.

All elastic waves in the ground rely for their existence and their speed of travel on the property of materials called elasticity. There are two fundamental kinds of elasticity. One relates to changes of volume without changes of shape, and the other to changes of shape without changes of volume. A convenient way of defining these is to specify the amount of force per unit area required to produce a given deformation. In other words, evaluate for each material the ratio stress/strain. Such a ratio is called an *elastic modulus*.

The *bulk modulus*, sometimes called the modulus of incompressibility, is

$$B = \frac{\text{stress}}{\text{strain}} = \frac{\text{increase in hydrostatic pressure}}{\text{change in volume per unit volume}}.$$

The *shear modulus*, or measure of resistance to change of shape, sometimes called the modulus of rigidity, is

$$G = \frac{\text{stress}}{\text{strain}} = \frac{\text{force per unit area}}{\text{shear}},$$

the shear being the angle through which a plane normal to the force is rotated.

Another, one of the earliest of the elastic moduli to be studied, is the modulus of stretch, known as *Young's modulus*, after Thomas Young, who is also known for his discovery of the interference of light. If a wire or rod of a material is stretched by a force acting parallel to its long axis, the length is changed. The modulus E (originally standing for elasticity) is then

$$E = \frac{\text{stress}}{\text{strain}} = \frac{\text{force per unit area}}{\text{change in length per unit length}}.$$

Elastic moduli, combined with the density, determine the velocity with which elastic waves travel in different materials. P-waves have a velocity which can be defined by the equation

$$V_p{}^2 = \frac{B + (4/3)\ G}{d};$$

for S-waves the velocity is given by

$$V_s{}^2 = \frac{G}{d}.$$

Among the surface waves, R-waves have a velocity that is of the order of $0.9\ V_s$ for the same material. Precise relations for the other surface waves have not been worked out. In general, C-waves are the first to pass a place near a source, H-waves are next, and Q-waves third, with R-waves last. This is illustrated in Fig. 36.

The conditions under which surface waves are generated by an underground explosion are quite varied, and may lead to the formation of only one type, or all, or different combinations of types.

Ordinarily, the meaning of "surface" in dealing with the

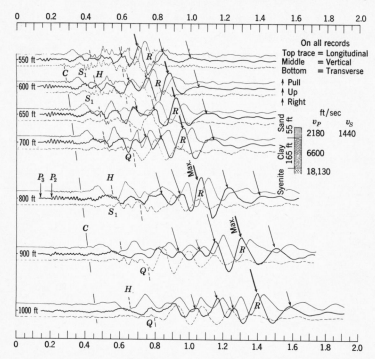

Fig. 36. Experimental profile illustrating wave types.

earth's surface is thought to be obvious. But with elastic surface waves, the word requires special definition. The waves themselves have a characteristic called wavelength, the distance between adjacent crests. The "surface" or region of material involved in the transmission of these waves is actually a zone about one wavelength in thickness. For many surface waves from dynamite blasts, this is of the order of 300 ft. For H-waves from the first atomic bomb, the zone of "surface" materials in which they were propagated was nearly 2500 ft thick.

All the elastic waves are generated in the same general region around an explosion at very nearly the same time; and all the motion of the earth's surface in the portions of the elastic zone closest to the charge is produced by the entire fraction of explosion energy that finds its way into elastic waves for distribution to more distant points. The energy is partitioned among the different types of waves that form, however, and these radiate downward and outward at different speeds until very quickly they have spread out to where they are separate groups. By then, the maximum motion of the ground surface is produced by the greatest motion in one wave type rather than by the total elastic wave energy. This can be seen developing in Fig. 36. As a result of this distribution of energy among different wave types, maximum ground motion decreases very rapidly at first, as distance from the explosion increases and the wave types separate. Once the wave types have separated, however, the ground motion they cause decreases at a less rapid rate as the individual waves die out from loss of energy and spreading out during their travel.

The rate at which elastic waves die out as they travel is determined by the nature of the materials through which they go. All rocks have higher elasticity than unconsolidated masses of sand, gravel, or clay, and transmit elastic waves more efficiently. In contrast, there are considerable frictional losses as waves move through unconsolidated materials, energy is rapidly exhausted by frictional conversion into heat, and the waves die out quickly. As a result, elastic waves carry their energy farther in rock than in unconsolidated material.

The corollary to this relation is that a given amount of wave energy causes much greater displacements of a surface of unconsolidated material with a thickness of half a wavelength or more than does the same energy in rock. This is what would be expected, if you consider the results of pushing with your hand and a pressure of, say, 10 lb/in.[2], first on a piece of granite then on a pile of sand. Of course, elastic waves deliver their energy by a very different mechanism, but the fact remains that a given pressure will displace a sand surface much more than a granite or other rock surface. Measurements have shown that an elastic wave of given energy may displace the surface of a thick mass of dry sand as much as 30 times as far as it displaces a surface of rock.

These differences are represented by numbers called *terrain coefficients*. A terrain coefficient expresses the ratio of actual ground displacement by elastic waves to that which the same waves would produce in rock. The terrain coefficient for rock is thus 1; for unconsolidated materials it ranges upward to as high as 30, depending on the thickness of the material. These relations are expressed in more detail on p. 112.

Waves in the Air

If an explosive is detonated in the open air, a shock front forms and moves into the air at supersonic speed. This is followed by the expanding hot gases of the explosion, also moving at supersonic speed. These are shown in Fig. 37.

At first, the pressure wave travels at high speed, but within a distance of about 20 to 50 times the diameter of the solid explosive its speed has leveled off at the speed of sound in air. From there, its travel is governed by air temperature, wind direction and speed, and such obstructions as buildings, vegetation, or hills.

Near the source, pressure waves in air from an explosion

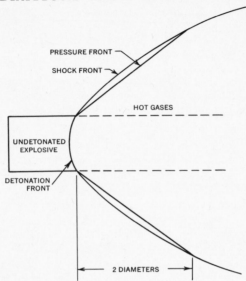

Fig. 37. Waves formed in air. (After M. A. Cook, by permission.)

have a wide range of frequencies, including the audible ones that produce sound effects. Most of the energy in such waves, however, is carried at frequencies less than 100 cycles per second, with peak intensities clustering between about 4 and 40 cycles per second. Lower frequencies carry to greater distances.

The peak pressure delivered to a given point by air waves from an explosion depends on the quantity of explosive, on whether it is exposed directly to air, on distance, and on weather conditions. Of these, weather conditions are so important that it is often difficult to isolate the other factors for study. During 1956 and 1957, however, an Explosives Research Group sponsored a series of studies that included blast surveys of 14 ordnance depots, from which extensive data established some of the general relations.[6] An indication of the order of magnitude of peak pressures of air waves is given in Table 9.

Table 9. Air-wave frequencies and pressures, measured simultaneously at 6,500 ft and 30,200 ft from TNT shots at Tooele Ordnance Depot under the same weather conditions.[a]

Weight of explosive	Dirt cover	Dominant frequency (cy/sec)		Peak Pressure (lb/in.^2)	
(lb)	(ft)	6,500 ft	30,200 ft	6,500 ft	30,200 ft
100	0	12	5.5	0.003	0.0002
1,000	2	10	4.2	.006	.0003
1,000	2	10	4.5	.008	.0002
5,000	6	8	—	.019	.0002
5,000	6	8	6.0	.023	.0001
10,000	10	—	5.5	.057	.0003

[a] From M. A. Cook, *The Science of High Explosives* (American Chemical Society Monogram No. 139; Reinhold, New York, 1958), p. 367.

It was found that a cover of even a few feet of dirt appreciably reduced the air-wave pressures. When the explosive is placed in boreholes in rock and covered by tamping, the air-wave pressures become literally negligible, though even then a loud noise may originate from uncovered Primacord or from explosion gases that escape directly to the air through joints.

Wide variations in the distribution of air-wave pressures around an explosion may result from meteorological conditions. In still air at constant temperature, the air waves go out in all directions at the same speed and with the same

[6] Summarized and discussed in M. A. Cook, *The Science of High Explosives* (American Chemical Society Monograph No. 139; Reinhold, New York, 1958).

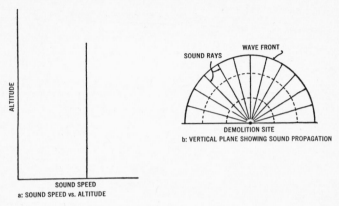

Fig. 38. Sound-wave fronts in still isothermal air. (After M. A. Cook, by permission.)

energy, as indicated in Fig. 38. If temperature and wind conditions cause the speed of sound to increase continuously with altitude, the wave fronts become warped and rays are the arcs of circles, as shown in Fig. 39. If sound velocity

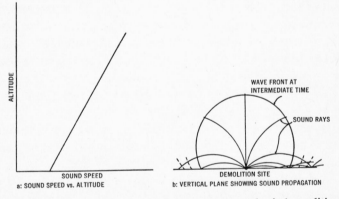

Fig. 39. Sound-wave fronts where temperature and wind conditions cause the sound velocity to increase continuously with altitude. (After M. A. Cook, by permission.)

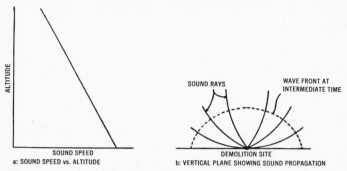

Fig. 40. Sound-wave fronts where the sound velocity decreases with altitude. No sound is heard along the ground. (After M. A. Cook, by permission.)

decreases with altitude, as is more often the case, the air waves curve upward and no sound is heard at distant points along the ground, as shown in Fig. 40.

If the speed of sound increases for a short distance upward, then decreases with height, a condition called a sound-speed inversion, air waves from an explosion return to the ground for a small distance only and do not reach greater distances. Other types of inversion cause correspondingly erratic distributions of air waves reaching different places on the ground surface.

Temperature distributions are by far the most important meteorological factors governing the travel of air waves from an explosion. Wind, however, can have an influence, too, when it contributes to the sound-velocity pattern. The nature of its effect is illustrated in Figs. 41 and 42.

A widely held belief that clouds confine sound by reflecting it back to the surface has not been borne out by controlled experiments. The cloud cover may be useful in forming an over-all picture of the environmental conditions affecting

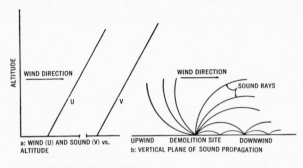

a: WIND (U) AND SOUND (V) vs. ALTITUDE   b: VERTICAL PLANE OF SOUND PROPAGATION

NOTE: V IS THE VELOCITY OF THE SOUND
WAVE RELATIVE TO THE EARTH ie.
$V = C + U$ (U = COMPONENT OF WIND IN
DIRECTION UNDER CONSIDERATION).

Fig. 41. Effect of wind on the travel of sound from an explosion. (After M. A. Cook, by permission.)

blast-wave propagation in air, but this is chiefly because clouds give clues to the temperature and wind conditions.

Recording Elastic Waves

An instrument for recording elastic waves is called a *seismograph*. A seismograph, of course, must rest on the ground or on a structure of which motion is to be recorded. The problem in designing a seismograph is to establish a reference point that either does not itself move, or else moves in some known manner different from the ground or structure.

The best way to meet this problem has been to build a seismograph around a weight, or inertia member, so supported by springs that when the base of the instrument moves the inertia member tends to remain at rest. Such an inertia member supported by springs has a natural frequency of vibration which depends on its weight and the stiffness of the springs. During the movement of its support by passing waves, the inertia member either remains at rest or moves

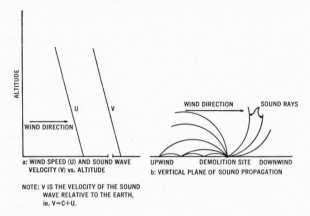

Fig. 42. Effect of wind on the travel of sound from an explosion. (After M. A. Cook, by permission.)

very little. Its behavior is governed by the ratio of the frequency of the earth waves to the natural frequency of the inertia member, and is called forced vibration.

Mathematical aspects of forced vibration have been discussed by many writers and the principles have been confirmed by many experiments.[7] The results can be summarized for our present purposes by terminology illustrated by Figs. 43–46 and a graph shown in Fig. 47.

Consider Fig. 43, in which a weight W is supported on frictionless and massless rollers; W is attached to a spring, which in turn is attached to the frame. Motion of W is described relative to this frame. The number of pounds required to extend the spring one inch is called the *spring constant*, and is represented by k.

If the weight W is displaced a small amount and then re-

[7] L. D. Leet, *Earth Waves* (Harvard Monographs in Applied Science, No. 2; Harvard University Press, Cambridge, 1950).

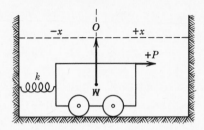

Fig. 43. Undamped linear vibratory system.

leased, it moves back and forth with simple harmonic motion of frequency f cycles per second given by

$$f = \frac{1}{2\pi} \left(\frac{kg}{W}\right)^{1/2},$$

where W is the weight in pounds and g is the accleration due to gravity, 386 in./sec^2.

At this point, we might pause to make a record of this

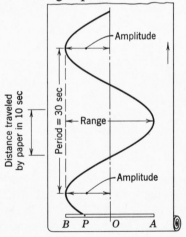

Fig. 44. Record of simple harmonic motion.

simple harmonic motion of the weight W in Fig. 44. Suppose P is a pen on the pointer of Fig. 43, moving with simple harmonic motion along the slot AB, with a strip of paper moving under this slot at constant speed. Then P traces on the paper a curve that records displacement as a function of time. From this curve, the amplitude and frequency of the motion can be measured, as indicated in the figure. It should be noted that the amplitude is the maximum displacement from the central position or position of no motion, O. The total distance AB through which the pointer moves is some-times called the double amplitude or range.

If a weight like that in Fig. 43 is to be used in a seismograph, something has to be done to prevent its oscillating freely once it has been disturbed. This involves bringing to bear on the system a force that resists the motion of W by an amount proportional to its velocity. Such a force is called *damping*. A dashpot is used for schematic representation of damping in Fig. 45, but in seismographs the damping is usually achieved by some variation of the principle that a copper vane or coil in motion in a magnetic field has currents in it which have their own magnetic fields that oppose the motion that caused them.

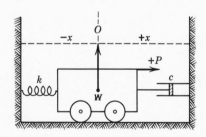

Fig. 45. Damped linear vibratory system.

A damping force that brings W to rest after one oscillation is called critical damping, and is represented by the symbol c_c. A weight serves best as a seismograph if it is damped about 0.6 critical. In other words, if c is the actual damping and c_c is critical damping, then a seismograph should have $c/c_c = 0.6$.

Now we are ready to set our weight W up as a seismograph and study its actions as it is subjected to forced vibrations of different frequencies. This is done in Fig. 46. We must first decide to measure the motion of W relative to its case as though we were inside the box watching, with no knowledge of what was going on outside. This is another way of saying that we measure displacements of W on axes that move with the case housing it. Then we place the case holding W on a base that moves. This might be the earth as elastic waves travel through it, or a building being vibrated by elastic waves. Motion of this base is described with reference to axes that are in imagination hung in space unmoved by disturbances of the seismograph's base. Further, let us

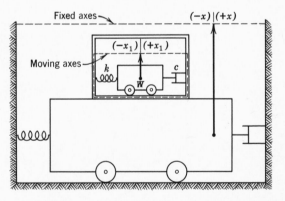

Fig. 46. Seismograph on a flexible moving structure.

represent motion of W in its case by x_1 and its maximum displacement by X_1, while motion of the base is x and its maximum displacement is X.

Solutions of the equations for this situation, supported by experiment, show that

$$X_1 = XZ,$$

where Z is a quantity called the *resonance factor*. Figure 47 shows a graph of Z as a function of f_e/f_0 for different amounts

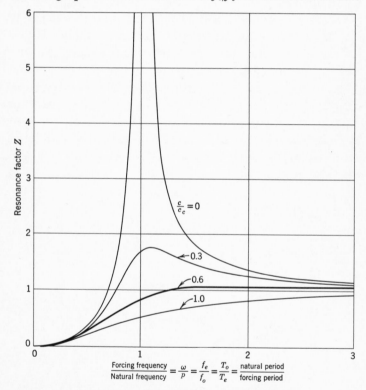

Fig. 47. Resonance factor for a damped system subjected to a force $P_0 \sin wt$.

of damping, where f_e is the frequency of the earth waves and f_0 is the natural frequency of W discussed above.

When the resonance factor is 1, W is recording most faithfully the motion of the earth or structure on which it rests. This actually means that W is standing still in space while the axes on which X_1 is measured move with the supporting structure. When there is no damping so that $c/c_c = 0$, if the earth-wave frequency equals the seismograph frequency, $f_e/f_0 = 1$, the curve for Z goes off the graph because the motion of W is very great under this condition, known as *resonance*. Resonance is a familiar phenomenon to anyone who has seen how giving a swing a little push each time it comes within reach will get it moving in a very large arc. This is the typical response when an outside force is applied to an undamped vibrating system at its natural frequency. Obviously, this would be an undesirable condition in a seismograph and it is for this reason that damping must be used. The curve in Fig. 47 for $c/c_c = 1$ represents critical damping, and the curve for $c/c_c = 0.6$ stays near $Z = 1$ over the widest range of frequency ratios.

From Fig. 47 we can see that W remains almost motionless in space, for the motion recorded in its case is nearly the same as the earth motion from $f_e/f_0 = 1$ to all larger values of this ratio. In other words, the seismograph is giving a record of the *displacement*.

For f_e/f_0 less than 1, the curves for Z at all damping ratios depart significantly from 1 as f_e/f_0 approaches zero. This means that W is no longer at rest in space and is doing some moving of its own. It has been found that for values of f_e/f_0 less than 0.5 the motion of W in its own case is actually proportional to the *acceleration* or rate of change of the earth motion, rather than the displacement. Under these

conditions, the seismograph is serving as an *accelerograph*.
The general relations in forced vibration can be demonstrated effectively by the use of a simple pendulum, as shown
in Fig. 48. With its point of support motionless, this pendulum

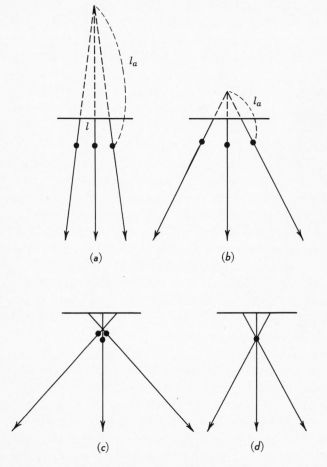

Fig. 48. Simple pendulum illustrating principles of forced vibration.

swings back and forth under the influence of gravity rather than springs, with a natural frequency

$$f_0 = \frac{1}{2\pi} \left(\frac{g}{l}\right)^{1/2},$$

where l is the length of the pendulum and g, as before, is the acceleration due to gravity. Now, move the point of support back and forth at a frequency f_e which is very small relative to the pendulum's natural frequency f_0. In other words, move the point of support very slowly. The pendulum bob will then move nearly the same amount as its support, and at the same frequency, much as though it were suspended from a point far above the level of its actual place of support, so that its apparent length l_a is much greater than l.

Next, move the support through the same amplitude, but at about the natural frequency f_0, and the phenomenon of resonance will be demonstrated as the pendulum bob swings as though hung from very nearly its actual point of support.

Then move the point of support again through the same amplitude, but this time at a greater frequency than f_0. Now the bob will move as though it were supported at a point between it and the true support. This point about which motion centers as forcing frequencies are changed is sometimes called the *center of oscillation*.

Finally, move the true point of support again through the same amplitude but at a frequency three or more times as great as f_0. Now, the cord or wire attached to the bob moves back and forth, but the bob remains at rest and simply rotates about its *center of gravity*. Here the center of gravity and center of oscillation coincide, and serve as a still point in space about which the rest of the system is moving.

Magnification

In a seismograph such as the one represented schematically by Fig. 46, if the natural frequency f_0 has been properly selected so that for earth waves that are to be recorded the inertia member is at rest in space, or nearly so, then a true record of displacements of the seismograph's base is written on the axes inside the seismograph's case. A practical difficulty arises, however, from the smallness of such displacements. They are commonly of the order of thousandths of an inch, and seldom exceed a few hundredths of an inch. So it is necessary to introduce a scheme for magnifying the displacements in order to record them.

Magnification of 50 times covers the greatest number of situations encountered in measuring waves from blasting rock. This can be achieved directly with invariable accuracy by a simple lever, such as the one indicated in Fig. 48 with the pendulum bob used to demonstrate forced vibration relations. As the bob, or inertia member of the pendulum, rotates about its center of gravity when the forcing frequency f_e is great enough. If a mirror is attached to the bob, a beam of light reflected from this mirror, becomes the long arm of a lever of which the pendulum bob is the fulcrum and the pendulum's supporting wire is the short arm. If the beam of light is allowed to fall upon photographic paper at a distant point, it traces an enlarged replica of the motion of the pendulum's support. The amount of enlargement is exactly the ratio of the long arm to the short arm of the lever.

This relatively straightforward aspect of seismographic instrumentation has sometimes been bypassed by designers who sought to obtain a compact package of convenient size by the use of mirrors on spindles rotated by nylon thread (but this changes its properties with humidity) or fine wire (but this is unable to stand the rigors of field usage and is also responsive to temperature changes). No compromise with the slightly cumbersome but completely simple and reliable direct lever has yet proved entirely satisfactory.

Recording System

The final step in seismographic instrumentation is a system for recording the motion. By far the commonest method is to record the motion from blasting vibrations on photographic paper or film, with reference marks to indicate time in some such convenient unit as hundredths of a second. The inertia systems that are best adapted to use in a seismograph for recording vibrations from blasting permit registration of motion in only one direction, so it is necessary to have three of them to obtain a full record of any general displacement. Two of these respond to horizontal motion in directions perpendicular to each other, and the third to vertical motion.

Leet Seismograph

The Leet seismograph is an example of a portable three-component seismograph designed primarily for the registration of vibrations from blasts, traffic, machinery, and general industrial sources. Each component has a natural frequency of 1 cycle per second. Magnetic damping is 0.6 critical. For frequencies above 3 c/sec, displacements are multiplied 50 times on the record. Timing lines are 0.01 sec apart.

A cutaway perspective view of the interior of this seismograph is shown in Fig. 49. The inertia members are suspended by flat springs; the spring for the vertical element is supplemented by a stabilizing coil spring. The horizontal components are at right angles to each other. The inertia element for one of the horizontal components is shown in detail in

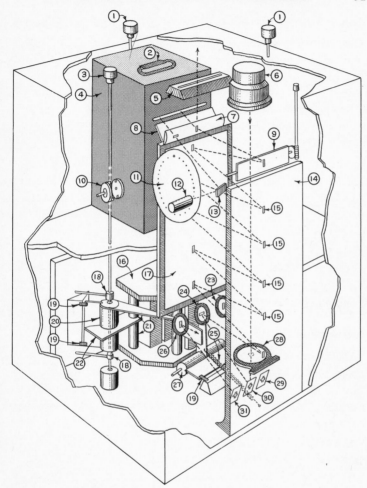

Fig. 49. Leet three-component portable seismograph: (1) knobs controlling leveling feet; (2) camera handle; (3) knob for locking inertia member; (4) camera; (5) viewing slit; (6) light-source housing; (7) cylindrical lens; (8) half-silvered mirror; (9) adjustable mirror; (10) camera-drive clutch; (11) timing-line shutter; (12) timing-line light housing; (13) timing-line mirror; (14) and (17) plane mirrors; (15) point of reflection; (16) permanent magnet; (18) locking nut; (19) spring; (20) and (27) inertia members; (21) magnet poles; (22) damping vane; (23), (24), and (26) inertia member mirrors; (25) stabilizing spring; (28) condensing lens; (29), (30), and (31) fixed mirrors.

Fig. 49. It consists of a cylindrical brass mass. Above and below it are plugs that close in on the cylinder and lock it for transportation when they are actuated by a knob on the top panel. Attached to the mass is a copper vane that swings between the extended poles of an Alnico magnet, for damping. Also attached to the mass is an arm which extends forward to support the concave mirror for that component so that it is in the same plane as the mirrors for the other elements.

Light is supplied by a straight-filament galvanometer lamp in a housing on the top panel. It travels directly to a condensing lens just above three fixed mirrors. The concave mirror attached to the inertia element for each of the horizontal components receives from its fixed mirror a rectangular patch of converging light, with the long axis vertical. It returns the light to the face of the outer of two long parallel plane mirrors. From this the light goes to the inner long mirror, and so on by eleven reflections to a cylindrical lens which brings it to a focus on the surface of the photographic paper in the camera for registration. The eleventh reflection is from a small mirror that can be adjusted about a horizontal axis.

The history of the light beam for the vertical component is slightly different, owing to the fact that the moving mirror for that component moves at right angles to those for the horizontal components, and without some correction its light would move up and down on the large plane mirrors instead of from side to side, as it must to record properly at the camera. To provide the correction, two prisms are interposed in the light path for the vertical component. Neither prism is shown in Fig. 49.

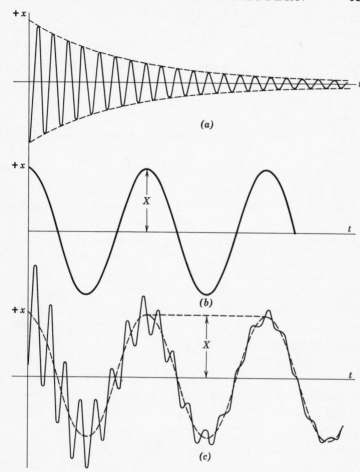

Fig. 50. Forced vibration: (*a*) free vibration, with angular frequency *p*, of the weight *W* of Fig. 45, with damping adjusted to cause an amplitude decrease of 10 percent per cycle, (*b*) steady-state vibration due to an applied force *P* with frequency $\omega = p/8$; (*c*) the actual motion — the sum of curves (*a*) and (*b*). (After Den Hartog.)

In principle, this seismograph is a simple mechanical-optical lever with a beam of light serving as a portion of the long arm of the lever. With the cover in place for carrying, the seismograph occupies a space $12 \times 14 \times 20$ in. and weighs 65 lb.

Interpretation of Seismograms

On the record from a displacement seismograph, deviations of a trace from its position when there is no vibration are directly proportional to true ground motion. With the Leet seismograph, for example, for frequencies within its range of 50 magnification each division on an engineering scale with 20 divisions to the inch represents 0.001 in. of true ground displacement. This relation can be applied directly and simply, however, only when a simple harmonic wave has been recorded by itself. When waves of more than one frequency are present on a record at the same time, great care and experience are required to assign the proper frequency to any measured amplitude. The principle is illustrated in Fig. 50 for two waves of different frequencies, where the higher is 8 times the lower. When we discuss ability to do damage, and the relation of energy or acceleration to this in a later section, we will find that these important factors vary as the square of the frequency of vibration. As a consequence, errors in reading which assign a given amplitude to the wrong frequency can be very serious indeed.

6

Safe Limits for Structures

We have seen how some of the energy from an explosion in rock escapes from the regions of shattering and plastic movement, to be carried to surrounding areas by elastic waves. Let us now consider some of the results when this energy reaches structures in the vicinity.

Mechanism of Movement

Energy can be delivered to a structure by flying missiles or by waves in the air or in the ground. The effect of the received energy on the structure is governed not only by its magnitude but also by the method of its delivery. In the case of waves, an important factor is the *wavelength*. For a wave that moves along the surface of the ground in a manner similar to the ever-convenient analogy of a wave on water, the greatest differences in position are between a particle on the crest of one wave and one in the trough of the next, half a wavelength away. Another way of stating this is to say that the greatest differential displacement is between points a half wavelength apart; and it is to be remembered that it is differential displacement that causes rupture of materials.

For example, pick up a yardstick. You can move it any amount you wish, so long as all its parts move together. But if you clamp one end to a table so it cannot move as you move the opposite end, the stick can be broken by a fairly small displacement of the free end relative to the fixed end, that is, by a differential displacement.

Now let us consider an elastic wave moving a structure in its path. If the wavelength is large relative to the size of the structure, the structure moves almost as a single unit, with very little differential displacement between any two points. Under these conditions, no materials in the structure are likely to be distorted enough to break.

The wavelength L is related to the velocity of the wave's travel V and its frequency f by the equation

$$L = \frac{V}{f}.$$

Most surface waves from blasting range in frequency from about 3 to 30 c/sec, and travel at velocities ranging from 1000 ft/sec in dry sand to 10,000 ft/sec in granite, with lower frequencies at lower velocities and the reverse. For example, if $V = 1000$ ft/sec and $f = 3$ c/sec, then $L = 333$ ft. Likewise, if $V = 10,000$ ft/sec and $f = 30$ c/sec, then $L = 333$ ft. A rough but practical rule, therefore, for estimating wavelength-to-structure-size ratios is to use a wavelength of 300 ft.

If a dwelling extends 30 ft in the path of such waves, no more than a tenth of any 300-ft wave would be under it at any instant, and the greatest differential displacement between parts of the dwelling would be 30/150 or a fifth of the range of the motion.

The sides of a buried pipe a foot in diameter, on the other

hand, would be exposed to no more than 1/150 of such a wave at any one instant. The pipe would move effectively as a unit with the ground and be exposed to literally negligible differential displacements.

Another important factor in determining the effect of elastic wave motion on structures is the frequency. Qualitatively, it is not difficult to see that moving a structure back and forth over a certain range would be more likely to damage it if the motion were reversed often in a second of time (high frequency) than if the motion were reversed at a relatively low rate (low frequency). Quantitatively, the importance of frequency stems from its contribution to the magnitudes of acceleration, force, and kinetic energy.

Acceleration is rate of change of motion in direction or amount, and force is mass times acceleration. Recall that the term mass as used here is numerically equal to weight divided by acceleration due to gravity. Kinetic energy is energy of motion, or a measure of the capacity of a body to do work as a consequence of its being in motion. Now, as an elastic wave passes a structure, the greatest acceleration to which the structure is subjected is

$$a_{max} = 4\pi^2 f^2 A,$$

where A is the amplitude. So the greatest force acting on the structure is its mass times this quantity, or

$$F_{max} = \frac{W}{g} a_{max} = \frac{W}{g} (4\pi^2 f^2 A),$$

where W is the weight in pounds and g is the acceleration due to gravity, 32.2 ft/sec^2 or 386 in./sec^2.

From this, it is clear that the force varies with the square of the frequency, and doubling the frequency quadruples the force.

Now, kinetic energy is

$$KE_{max} = \frac{1}{2} \frac{W}{g} v_{max}^2,$$

where v is the velocity with which a structure moves back and forth as waves pass it. Since

$$v_{max} = 2\pi f A,$$

then

$$v_{max}^2 = 4\pi^2 f^2 A^2.$$

Thus we again find a quantity, this time kinetic energy, which is proportional to the square of the frequency, with the result that doubling the frequency quadruples the kinetic energy.

Damage Criteria

Fundamentally, the property of wave motion that governs effects on structures is the energy which the waves deliver to the structure, though this may be represented by the amplitude of the motion it produces, the frequency of the motion, the acceleration which results from combining the amplitude and frequency, the force with which it moves a structure, or the energy itself, defined in terms of the velocity of the motion it produces. All these quantities are subject to direct measurement and various combinations of them have been used as numbers against which conditions of damage or no damage were examined.

Frequency and amplitude are the basic elements of

harmonic motion, from which others can be computed. As
pointed out above, if f is frequency and A is amplitude, then

$$\text{acceleration} = a = (4\pi^2)(f^2 A),$$

$$\text{force} = ma = \frac{W}{g}(4\pi^2)(f^2 A),$$

$$\text{velocity} = v = (2\pi)(fA),$$

$$\text{kinetic energy} = \frac{Wv^2}{2g} = \frac{W}{2g}4\pi^2(f^2 A^2).$$

The way in which these elements of harmonic motion vary
is illustrated by Table 10. This table shows that the maximum

**Table 10. Elements of simple harmonic motion
for waves from different sources**

Source	f (c/sec)	A (in.)	a in./sec²	Ratio of a	f^2A^2	KE	Ratio of KE
Walking	22	0.0036	69	1.9	0.0063	0.000326W	.8
Blast	10	0.0090	36	1	0.0080	.000410W	1
Quake	1.3	1.42	101	2.8	3.6300	.185000W	450

acceleration, hence the maximum force, caused by the earthquake was only 2.8 times that computed for the quarry blast,
but the maximum kinetic energy was 450 times as much.
The blast vibrations did no damage of any kind, but the
earthquake vibrations did a great deal of damage.

A factor not represented by any computations of maximum
values for acceleration, kinetic energy, or other measures is
total energy, which is governed also by the duration of
significant motion. This is a fraction of a second for blast
vibrations, but may be many minutes for earthquake waves
near their source.

Observations and computations of this kind have led to the conclusion that the best guide to damage-causing possibilities of vibrations is the energy they are found to possess. Since it is neither practicable nor necessary to determine the energy in inch pounds, which would involve knowing or computing the weights of structures being shaken, energy from a particular source is compared with energies from other sources by determining the square of the velocity which each source produces at a point on the ground or in a structure.

Kinetic energy is proportional to v^2, so ratios of kinetic energy are computed directly by determining ratios of v^2. Rockwell [1] pointed this out in 1927, and later Crandell [2] utilized the relation in defining his "energy ratio":

$$ER = \frac{a^2}{f^2},$$

where a is acceleration and f is frequency. Examination of the dimensions of Crandell's "energy ratio" shows that it is proportional to $f^2 A^2$, which makes it proportional to v^2, hence to kinetic energy.

The U.S. Bureau of Mines, as part of an extensive study of vibrations from blasting, with particular reference to their capacity for damaging plaster, reported effects as a function of acceleration.[3] Their results contributed greatly to our knowledge of relations between damage to property and

[1] E. H. Rockwell, *Vibrations Caused by Blasting and Their Effect on Structures* (Hercules Powder Co., Wilmington, Delaware, 1931).

[2] F. J. Crandell, "Ground Vibration Due to Blasting and Its Effect Upon Structures," *J. Boston Soc. Civ. Engs. 36*, 222–245 (1949).

[3] J. R. Thoenen and S. L. Windes, *Seismic Effects of Quarry Blasting* (U.S. Bureau of Mines, Bulletin 442; Government Printing Office, Washington, 1942).

vibrations from blasting, and they also demonstrated that acceleration is not well adapted to service as a criterion of damage from such vibrations. They reported as a zone of "caution" accelerations between 0.1g and g, with damage not statistically expectable until the acceleration exceeds that due to gravity. This appeared at first glance to be in conflict with experience in earthquake areas, where accelerations of the order of 0.1g were often the threshold of damage. However, there is no real conflict between the two categories of damage from blast vibrations and damage from earthquakes. The trouble lies entirely in the inadequacy of acceleration as a criterion of damage. There can be no damage in any case unless there is sufficient energy, no matter what numerical values are computed for such a property of vibratory motion as acceleration. In this connection, you might look again at Table 10, where earthquake vibrations that did extensive damage showed a maximum acceleration less than 3 times that of blast vibrations that did no harm of any kind. On the other hand, the earthquake vibrations had more than 450 times as much maximum kinetic energy as the blast vibrations and — not shown on the table at all — several thousand times the total energy and duration of significant vibration.

Safe Limits of Elastic Vibration

The U.S. Bureau of Mines, from 1935 to 1940, conducted tests at 28 stone quarries, a limestone mine, and 20 residential structures of various types. Included among the objectives of this program was determination of the amount of vibration necessary to damage structures. "Damage" was defined as damage to plaster, since this is the weakest material in structures where it is used. Results were reported in Bulletin 442 referred to above.

During the five years, though hundreds of observations were made of the nature and effects of elastic vibrations from commercial blasting at the quarries and mine, no damage was observed. So two procedures were followed. Special test blasting was conducted near a house until damage was done, and a heavy rotating mechanical shaker was used to vibrate other structures until damage occurred. In these ways, certain numbers were obtained for the amount and kind of vibration that actually caused known damage under conditions of careful observation. The shaker tests were not truly representative of vibrations such as come from blasting, because their duration was appreciably greater, but at the time they were conducted they gave the first quantitative clues in this problem.

Crandell reported an extensive series of instrumental measurements supplemented by detailed building inspections, where blasting was carried on near homes, schools, and churches. Many cases of damage were encountered, and many more where there was no damage. Crandell concluded that "when the structure had not been prestressed and the materials of construction were average, no damage occurred" if the energy ratio was less than 3. In some structures where there had been prestressing and cracking by settlement or movement of any sort, an energy ratio of 3 or greater sometimes increased the width of cracks previously formed. He summarized his experience by defining the region between energy ratios of 3 and 6 as "caution," and greater than 6 as "danger" for structures. These are plotted in Fig. 51 as a function of frequency and amplitude of vibration.

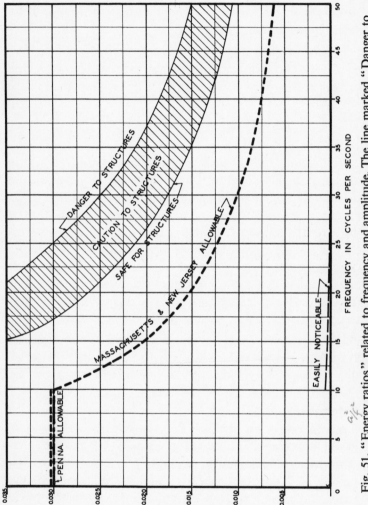

Fig. 51. "Energy ratios" related to frequency and amplitude. The line marked "Danger to structures" represents an energy ratio of 6; that marked "Safe for structures," an energy ratio of 3; the dotted line marked "Massachusetts and New Jersey allowable" represents an energy ratio of 1 down to a frequency of 10 c/sec.

Perceptibility

An extremely important factor in this whole problem has been the discovery that vibrations can be felt by people, and may even seem severe, when their amplitude is only a fraction of that necessary to do damage.[4] This is demonstrated in the graph of Fig. 51.

Vibrations from Normal Use

Vibrations from normal use of structures provide a helpful reference level against which to compare vibrations from blasting. Of course, walking on a floor does not always shake an entire house, though slamming a door often does. But the materials of a floor, ceiling, or wall panel of a single room do not know or care whether vibrations to which they are subjected come from that room only or from a distant point outside the house, and their response to measured vibrations from normal use is a practical guide to their capacity to withstand vibrations from other sources. Displacements of 0.010 or 0.020 in., or more, at frequencies of from 5 to 20 c/sec are not uncommon in dwelling structures from walking, door slamming, and other activities of the occupants.

Potential Crater Zone

In our discussion of craters formed by the detonation of buried explosives, we defined a region called the potential crater zone (p. 52). This is the region in which, if a sufficient quantity of explosive were used, the rock would be shattered and projected outward to form a crater. The size of the crater

---

[4] H. Reiher and F. J. Meister, "Die Empfindlichkeit des Menschen gegen Erschütterungen (Human Sensitivity to Vibration)," *Forsch. Gebiete Ingenieurw.* 2, 381–386 (1931).

depends critically on the depth at which the explosive is buried and on the type of rock. Even though no crater is formed, the rock movements within the potential crater zone are in general not the simple elastic oscillations involved in setting the safe limits for vibration that we have just discussed. They often include permanent plastic displacements. For many brittle rocks, the diameter of the potential crater zone is not greatly different from twice the depth at which the explosive is buried, but it is a dimension that cannot be predicted with precision at the present time without instrumental measurements. Permanent displacement is indicated by a shift in the zero position of the inertia members of a Leet seismograph, if the ground tilts at the recording location, or by failure of a strain gauge to return to a position of no strain, as at short distances in Figs. 30–33.

Fixed safe limits for permanent displacement depend on each individual structure and on the parts of the structure which are supported by the ground thus affected. The best advice that can be given at present to insure safety from effects within a potential crater zone is: *keep buildings or other earth-supported materials such as pipelines out of it.*

7

Observations and Applications

Appearance and Mechanism of Well-Drilled-Quarry or Open-Pit Shots

A good example of the sequence and results of reflection rupture and burden movement is found in a quarry or open-pit blast where explosives are loaded in vertical holes aligned parallel to the face and detonated in continuous sequence by a millisecond-delay technique.

The powder factor, sometimes called the loading ratio, or number of tons of stone most efficiently shattered by a pound of explosive, together with the area blocked out by boreholes prepared to hold the explosive, determines the total amount of explosive loaded for a blast. For instance, if a 125-ft-high face of limestone is to be blasted for a distance of 100 ft along the face, using holes 20 ft back from the face, that is, a burden of 20 ft, the total volume of rock to be broken would be $125 \times 100 \times 20 = 250,000$ ft^3. At approximately 12 ft^3/ton, this represents nearly 21,000 tons of rock. For a powder factor of 4, that is, where 4 tons of rock are satisfactorily broken by 1 lb of explosive, the total weight of explosive required for such a blast would be 5250 lb. This would be distributed among the boreholes so that the greatest

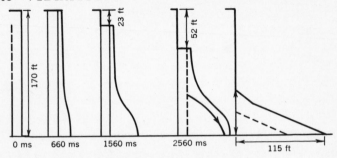

Fig. 52. Profile of a quarry face 660, 1560, and 2560 ms after a blast, and broken stone afterward. (After Deffet and Boutry.)

explosive energy was concentrated in the lower parts of the holes, and inert tamping material would be used to fill each hole above the column of explosive. For best breakage and smallest vibration, such holes are detonated by millisecond delays starting at one end of the line of holes and progressing continuously along the line.

High-speed photographs of a face during a blast of this general type have shown how a reference point and the general rock mass moved, and where the broken rock reposed after the blast.[1] A schematic section through a blast hole is shown in Fig. 52, where the shape of the face is indicated after intervals of 0.660, 1.560, and 2.560 sec following initiation of detonation, as well as the shape of the final pile of broken stone. The toe, or lower portion of the face, moved out at an average speed of 25 ft/sec, and the upper portion of the face simply collapsed as support was removed from it. Fragmentation by the reflected shock front could not be recognized in the photographs, but was completed within 10 to 15 milliseconds.

[1] L. Deffet and C. Boutry, "Etude Cinematographique de Tirs en Masse," *Explosifs 10*, 41–52 (1957).

Figures 53–59 are sequence pictures of a basalt quarry face as 5150 lb of explosive fired by millisecond delays broke 24,000 tons of rock. These show the bottom part moving out and top dropping as diagramed in Fig. 52.

Shortly after this shot was photographed, a small greenhouse was erected on the floor of this quarry 100 yd in front of the face, for test purposes. During succeeding years of operation of the quarry with shots similar to that of Figs. 53–59 there was no glass broken in this greenhouse, either by missiles or by concussion.

Vibrations Related to Quantity of Explosive and Distance

One of the results of the extensive experiments by the U.S. Bureau of Mines [2] was development of an empirical formula relating maximum displacement by vibrations to quantity of explosive and distance.

[2] J. R. Thoenen and S. L. Windes, *Seismic Effects of Quarry Blasting* (U.S. Bureau of Mines, Bulletin 442; Government Printing Office, Washington, 1942).

Fig. 53. Quarry face before a blast. (Photo by Atlas Powder Company.)

Fig. 54. Quarry face of Fig. 53 starting to move after detonation of explosives. (Photo by Atlas Powder Company.)

Fig. 55. Later stage in movement of quarry face of Fig. 53. (Photo by Atlas Powder Company.)

Fig. 56. Outward movement of bottom of face is pronounced. Large blocks near top have started to drop. (Photo by Atlas Powder Company.)

Fig. 57. Later stage of movement. (Photo by Atlas Powder Company.)

Fig. 58. Movement of rock nearing completion. (Photo by Atlas Powder Company.)

Fig. 59. The pile of broken material after the shot. (Photo by Atlas Powder Company.)

As has been pointed out (p. 75), the actual amount of motion in the ground depends not only on quantity of explosive and distance but also on the nature of the terrain at the point in question. With the shaking produced by a wave at a given point on rock assigned a coefficient of 1, it has been observed that the same wave at the same point would shake or displace 10 times as much the surface of average overburden (about a quarter to a half wavelength thickness of unconsolidated soil or earth lying on rock). Accordingly, normal overburden is said to have a *terrain coefficient* of 10. Abnormal overburden (half a wavelength or more in thickness) of water-soaked sand, or dry sand, gravel, and loam, may have a terrain coefficient as high as 30. Overburden a few feet in thickness has no appreciable effect on the terrain coefficient, which is therefore 1 at such a point.

This terrain coefficient should not be confused with the effect of different earth materials in damping out or absorbing the energy of elastic waves (p. 74).

In developing the formula relating quantity of explosive, distance, and maximum amplitude of elastic-wave motion, the Bureau of Mines averaged results for waves transmitted over a great variety of terrains in different parts of the country, so variations in transmission efficiency are averaged into the results. The formula was then computed for average overburden at the recording points. Accordingly, amplitudes computed by the formula are multiplied by 3 for a receiving point located on abnormal overburden, or divided by 10 for one located on rock, or close to it.

A very important feature of the decrease in maximum amplitude of earth motion caused by elastic waves as distance from their source increases is the separation of wave types by their velocity differences, discussed and illustrated

Table 11. Amplitude (in.) of ground motion for normal overburden and various weights of explosives and distances from the shot [a]

Weight of explosive (lb)	Distance from shot (ft)										
	500	600	700	800	900	1000	2000	3000	4000	5000	6000
100	0.0076	0.0066	0.0059	0.0050	0.0044	0.0038	0.0011	0.0004	0.0003	0.0002	0.0002
500	.022	.019	.017	.015	.013	.011	.0032	.0013	.0008	.0006	.0006
1,000	.035	.031	.027	.023	.020	.018	.0050	.0020	.0012	.0010	.0010
2,000	.056	.049	.044	.037	.032	.028	.0080	.0032	.0019	.0016	.0016
3,000	.073	.064	.057	.048	.042	.037	.010	.0042	.0025	.0021	.0021
4,000	.089	.078	.069	.059	.051	.045	.013	.0051	.0030	.0025	.0025
5,000	.100	.090	.080	.068	.059	.052	.015	.0058	.0035	.0029	.0029
6,000	.120	.100	.090	.076	.067	.058	.016	.0066	.0040	.0033	.0033
7,000	.130	.110	.100	.085	.074	.065	.018	.0073	.0044	.0036	.0036
8,000	.140	.120	.110	.093	.081	.071	.020	.0080	.0048	.0040	.0040
9,000	.150	.130	.120	.100	.088	.076	.022	.0086	.0052	.0043	.0043
10,000	.160	.140	.130	.110	.094	.082	.023	.0093	.0056	.0046	.0046

[a] From U.S. Bureau of Mines Bulletin 442, p. 66. For rock or very thin overburden, divide the tabulated amplitudes by 10; for abnormal overburden (thicker than 50 ft.), multiply by 3.

on p. 74. As a practical matter, this separation is accomplished within about the first 500 ft. After that, the decrease in maximum amplitude is controlled by the rate at which the one wave type producing it has died out. As a result, the rate of amplitude decrease, on the average, follows one law out to, say, 500 ft. and another beyond that.

For total weight of explosives from 1000 through 10,000 lb and distances from 500 to 6000 ft, the Bureau of Mines found that the following formula expresses the maximum amplitude of elastic-wave motion on normal overburden:

$$A = \frac{C^{2/3}}{100} (0.07e^{-0.00143d} + 0.001),$$

where A (in. is the maximum resultant amplitude, C (lb) is the weight of the explosive charge, d (ft) is the distance, and e is the base of natural logarithms (2.72).

Table 11 shows values for A calculated from this formula.

The Bureau of Mines formula predicts amplitudes that are increasingly greater than those observed as the amount of explosive rises above 10,000 lb. For example, at 1500 ft from 76,000 lb the formula predicts an amplitude of 0.161 in. for normal overburden or 0.016 for rock. An actual observation on rock showed an amplitude of 0.011 in. At 8000 ft from 1,362,985 lb, the formula predicts an amplitude of 1.200 in. on normal overburden or 0.120 on rock. An actual record on rock showed an amplitude of 0.027 in. It is reproduced in Fig. 60, and a record of the same blast at 11,500 ft is shown in Fig. 61. Photographs of the shot are shown in Figs. 62–64.

In Chapter 6, we found that frequency is an important factor in determining damage. The amplitude-distance-quantity equation and table do not involve frequency, but

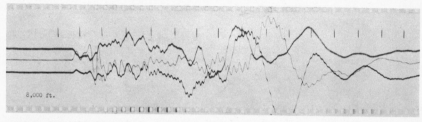

Fig. 60. Ground displacements 8000 ft. from a 0.7-kiloton (1,362,985-lb) blast by TVA at South Holston, Tennessee, February 5, 1949; maximum amplitude, 0.027 in. (Recorded on a Leet seismograph by L. Don Leet.)

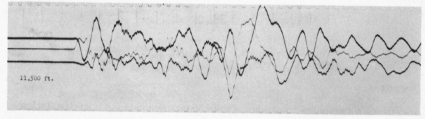

Fig. 61. Ground displacements at 11,500 ft from the South Holston blast; maximum amplitude, 0.018 in. (Recorded on a Leet seismograph by Jules Jenkins.)

certain general ranges of frequency have been observed and can be used to make helpful estimates of damage potential from these amplitudes. Higher frequencies are observed on rock, often ranging from 25 to 50 c/sec. Maximum motion is associated with lower frequencies on overburden, often ranging from 3 to 5 c/sec for the thickest overburdens. Another relation is that large quantities of explosive produce maximum motions in elastic waves associated with lower frequencies than do smaller quantities in the same terrain. In other words, the frequency at maximum elastic-wave amplitudes varies inversely as the quantity of explosive.

Fig. 62. Hill near South Holston, Tennessee, where TVA placed 1,362,985 lb of Nitramon and primers in a mile of tunnels to break more than 1,800,000 tons of rock for a dam. (Photo courtesy E. I. du Pont de Nemours and Company)

Fig. 63. The hill of Fig. 62 shortly after detonation of the explosives.

Fig. 64. The hill of Fig. 62 after the blast.

Tunneling Through Rock

Tunneling through rock involves special procedures in drilling and blasting, and produces vibration patterns that are unique.

Tunnels for water-supply, sewer, or utility purposes are usually small enough — up to 10 or 15 ft in diameter — that the full face or heading is worked on each blast. Boreholes 2 in. or so in diameter are drilled parallel to the line of the tunnel, to lengths of 8 or 10 ft. Explosives in these holes are detonated in sequence so that the center of the tunnel is taken out first, and the rock around it breaks into this relieved region. Long delays separating detonations by a second or more have been used in this service for many years.

Vibrations at the surface immediately or almost immediately above such tunneling operations are essentially confined to body waves. The first or "cut" round causes the largest vibration because, in blasters' terminology, it is "tight.". Seismologically, this is a condition in which the shock front from the cut round has much less area of free face over which to use its energy in shattering rock than do later shock fronts in the same sequence. Figure 65 shows vibrations on the surface 100 ft above and 25 ft to one side of the centerline of a 13-ft tunnel, from a shot fired in nine rounds, now usually called delays. The total quantity of explosive was 113 lb and the greatest amount of one delay was 12.5 lb.

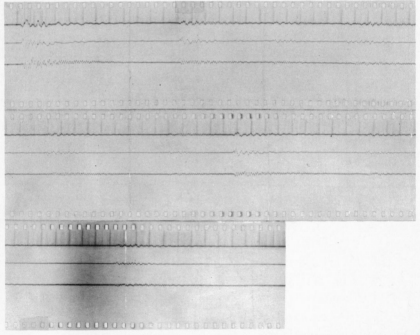

Fig. 65. Ground displacements 100 ft above and 25 ft to one side of a tunnel shot totaling 113 lb fired in nine delays, with 12.5 lb each. (Courtesy Dravo Corporation.)

The diameter of such a tunnel automatically limits the amount of explosive that can be loaded at any one time, and it usually works out that it would be impossible to load sufficient explosives fired in sequence like this to damage structures on the surface without destroying the tunnel itself. The vibrations shown in Fig. 65 were recorded during the driving of a sewer tunnel that went directly under part of the Golden Triangle in the heart of Pittsburgh, Pennsylvania, without damage to structures. In fact, the vibrations on the surface from this tunneling operation were generally smaller than those from traffic and industry in the area, and less harmful to dwellings than vibrations from normal use.

Vibrations Generated by Millisecond-Delay Detonation

Separation of detonation into a series of independent events by delay firing has spectacularly reduced the by-product vibrations, even though this separation is by no more than a few milliseconds. An understanding of the mechanism by which this reduction is achieved is important to a full use of the method, and has been gained through instrumental records.

At the source, vibrations that ultimately reach surrounding ground are generated by the shock front from any given package of explosives. The elastic waves that produce the greatest motion observed at a distance come into being when this shock front hits the nearest surface of the ground. The energy that goes into such waves depends directly on the energy in the shock front that generates them. So when delay detonation splits into separate bundles the total amount of explosive energy in a blast, it likewise splits into separate bundles the energy with which the shock fronts hit the surface and set up elastic waves for travel to distant points.

The reality of this division of the energy is illustrated by Fig. 66. This record shows acceleration of the ground 400 ft from a blast fired with five delays, at intervals of 0.025 sec. Since force is mass times acceleration, this record in effect shows the distribution in time of the force applied to the ground at the surface recording point, the force that generated elastic waves for travel to surrounding areas. The ground was struck five separate and distinct blows, each of an amount produced by the explosive detonated on one delay.

The result of this is that the maximum vibration at distant points is that which has been generated by the greatest amount of explosive fired at any one instant. This is conveniently referred to as the *maximum per delay*.

An example of the effect at a more distant point of such

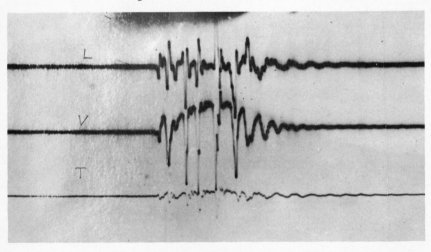

Fig. 66. Record of acceleration 400 ft from a blast fired in five delays; *L* designates the longitudinal component, *V* the vertical, and *T* the transverse. (Recorded on a Knobel accelerograph by L. Don Leet.)

millisecond separation of impacts is shown in Fig. 67. The top record of that figure shows displacements at a distance of 2500 ft from 41,425 lb of explosive detonated instantaneously in a tunnel blast. The maximum resultant displacement (M.R.D.) was 0.0317 in. The same seismograph at the same location produced the second record from 44,434 lb of explosive loaded in 20 9-in. holes and detonated by millisecond delays. The maximum resultant displacement in that case was 0.0021 in. or one-fifteenth of the amount produced by less explosive fired instantaneously.

The intervals by which millisecond delays separate the

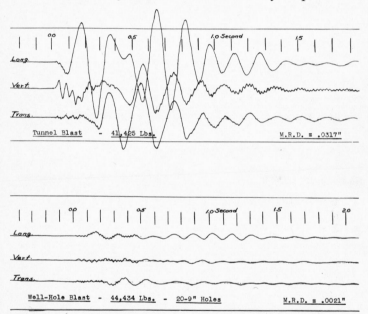

Fig. 67. Effect of millisecond-delay firing in reducing ground motion at a distance of 2500 ft. (Recorded on a Leet seismograph by Ranald Jones.)

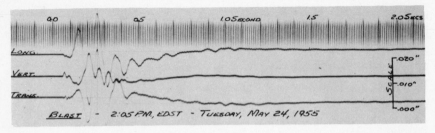

Fig. 68. Effect of delay interval on reduction of vibrations by millisecond detonation. The top record shows ground amplitudes 1000 ft from 1790 lb maximum per delay, with delay interval of 9 ms. The bottom record shows ground amplitudes at the same place from 1720 lb per delay, with delay interval of 17 ms.

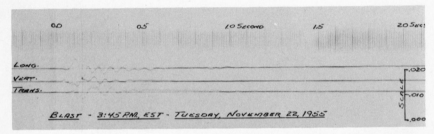

detonations of groups of explosives can vary considerably, but for every rock there is some value below which reduction of vibration becomes less pronounced. There must also be a balance of sorts among delay interval, hole spacing, and burden. For example, if an effective delay interval in a certain rock is about 1 millisecond per foot of hole spacing, intervals less than half this are likely to be much less successful in reducing vibrations. An illustration of this can be found in Fig. 68. The top record in this figure shows ground amplitudes 1000 ft from a blast loaded with a maximum of 1790 lb per delay and a delay interval of 9 milliseconds. The bottom record shows ground amplitudes at the same place for a maximum of 1720 lb per delay, but a delay interval of 17 ms. In this case, the optimum interval for the type of rock and customary hole spacing was around 25 ms. The use of a 17-ms interval did not seriously reduce the effectiveness in reducing vibration, but a 9-ms interval was definitely too short.

Effect of Millisecond Delays on Breakage

There is a close connection between the reduction of vibration by millisecond detonation and the breakage, or extent to which rock is broken into sizes convenient for removal. In effect, vibrations in the ground around a blast carry leftover or wasted energy that was not used in breaking rock when the explosives were detonated. As a result, if breakage is incomplete, vibrations are larger than they would have been if more energy had gone into producing better breakage.

The exact mechanism by which delays improve breakage is not known. It is likely, however, that an important factor is that shock fronts and expanding gases from late-firing holes operate into large numbers of free faces produced by energy from the earlier holes that would not have been available if all the holes had fired together.

Figure 69 shows a striking difference in breakage by two adjacent shots of similar total explosives, number of holes, and hole spacing, where one was fired instantaneously and the other by delays.

Vibrations from Normal Use of Buildings

Every structure is subjected to vibrations from normal use. Walking, slamming doors, moving furniture, and similar activities of people cause them. Rotating machinery, such as

Fig. 69. Breakage from delay shot (*left*) and instantaneous shot (*right*) of similar total explosives and number of holes. (Photo courtesy L. F. Miller.)

an automatic washing machine, is a powerful source in many cases. It is common for such "normal" vibrations to be greater than those to which buildings are exposed in the vicinity of blasting operations. Figure 70 illustrates an example where this comparison was made.

Underwater Blasting

When explosives are loaded in boreholes and procedures are otherwise essentially similar to those on land, the presence of water over a shot has no effect on vibrations in the ground from the blasting. On the other hand, shock pressures that reach water surrounding the blast are transmitted through it much more efficiently than through air, and occasionally represent a threat to nearby structures.

A special case of this type has been encountered when a rock plug has to be blasted from a canal or water-tunnel entrance close to existing dam or powerhouse installations. In one such instance, a power company averted a million-

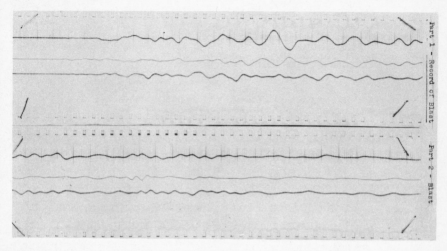

Fig. 70. Vibrations in a dwelling-house living room. The top two records show vibrations from a quarry shot 2500 ft away. The bottom record shows the effect of stamping a foot 3 ft from the seismograph in the same location.

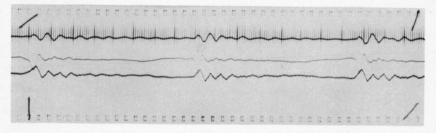

dollar shutdown of ten generators by spending about $2000 to put a curtain of air bubbles between a 12,000 lb blast and a powerhouse 250 ft away. A 6-in. air line was connected to three perforated 3-in. pipes laid along the bottom adjacent to the shot and clamped 9 in. apart. Compressed air under 90 lb/in.^{2} of pressure was pumped into the pipes at 3700 ft^3/min. Air bubbles from the pipe perforations raised the surface of the water 4 ft above normal and so disrupted the elastic continuity of the water that no significant pressures reached the powerhouse.

Is Soil Compacted by Elastic Vibrations from Blasting?

Explosives have been used for the compaction of soil under very special conditions.[3] This basic fact has become in some instances the foundation for a line of "reasoning" that neglects the special conditions and details of procedure actually involved, then jumps to completely unsupported speculations about elastic waves from blasting causing compaction in strong, cohesive soils at remote distances.

Explosives can be used for soil compaction, according to Lyman, "only if a new and denser soil structure will be formed after the material is completely disturbed." Requirements for compacting loose, cohesionless foundation soils in their natural state by detonating buried explosives include having the soil saturated. The method has been successful on loose deposits of uniformly graded, slightly silty, fine to medium saturated sands. The size of the charge must be such as to "shatter the soil mass thoroughly." Good results were obtained from 8-lb charges spaced 20 ft on centers and buried 15 ft. The effects were produced only within the range of direct application of explosives pressures to cause permanent displacements, and ceased where the ground motion was entirely that of elastic waves.

Compaction of granular soils is also accomplished by

[3] A. K. B. Lyman, "Compaction of Cohesionless Foundation Soils By Explosives," *Trans. Am. Soc. Civil Engrs.* 107, 1330 (1942).

mechanical vibration and simultaneous saturation with water in a process known as "vibroflotation." [4,5] The force in this method is applied by a device called a vibroflot. This is a long, slender tube of which one part is a 6-ft long section, 15 in. in diameter, containing the vibrator that drives a 200-lb eccentric $1\frac{1}{4}$ in. off center at 1800 rev/min, developing a centrifugal force of 10 tons and maximum movement of the bottom of the vibroflot of $\frac{3}{4}$ in. The process relies on mechanical agitation and simultaneous saturation with water to move and "float" the sand particles into a dense state. The vibrations are effective to a radial distance of 5 to 8 ft.

With vibroflotation as with explosives, compaction is achieved only within the range where the sand or granular material is saturated and the forces are sufficient to produce permanent displacements.

In contrast to these established methods for compacting *saturated* sands by explosives or "vibrations," within a few feet of the energy sources, there is overwhelming evidence from both theory and actual observation that there is no compaction of soils from elastic waves outside the potential crater zone from blasting rock.

State and Other Regulations Limiting Vibrations

On August 8, 1952, the Department of Labor and Industry for the state of New Jersey promulgated rules and regulations governing quarry blasting and related operations. These

[4] Elio D'Appolonia, "Loose Sands — Their Compaction By Vibroflotation," American Society for Testing Materials, Special Technical Publication No. 156 (1953).

[5] Elio D'Appolonia and C. E. Miller, Jr., "Sand Compaction By Vibroflotation," *Trans. Am. Soc. Civil Engrs. 120*, 154 (1955).

contained a section on allowable limits for seismic effects and air blast, prefaced by the statement that "Allowable limits of ground motion and sound pressure contained in this section shall be considered neither to produce structural damage in any structure that has been reasonably well constructed according to accepted engineering practice nor to constitute a nuisance to persons." The allowable limits varied with frequency so that an "energy ratio" of 1 would not be exceeded at any building not owned by the quarry (Table 12).

Table 12. Amplitudes of ground motion at different frequencies, produced when the "energy ratio" is 1.

Frequency (c/sec)	Maximum amplitude (in.)
10	0.0305
20	.0153
30	.0102
40	.0076
50	.0061
60	.0051

These limits were later imposed on blasting in New Jersey for any purpose, and were also set by the state of Massachusetts. The same limits were imposed by the Port Authority of the State of New York upon all contractors blasting in connection with the Niagara Power Project, on which construction began early in 1958, and by the U.S. Army Corps of Engineers on blasting for channel excavation in the Delaware River, begun in the latter half of 1958. Both the Port Authority of New York and the Corps of Engineers incorporated in their specifications stipulations that contractors supply and operate seismographs during the blasting, to establish conformity with the vibration limitations.

Of the several damage criteria discussed earlier, it was pointed out that the "energy ratio" appeared to be the most realistic. Experiment demonstrated that "energy ratios" less than 3 are safe, when damage to plaster as the weakest material in a structure is the consideration. So when New Jersey and the organizations following the same pattern set an "energy ratio" of 1 as the highest allowable at structures outside a blast area, they introduced a safety factor. In terms of "energy ratio," this safety factor is 3. In terms of quantities of explosive, however, it is much greater. Recall, for example, that "energy ratio" is proportional to the square of the amplitude. Accordingly, if we are to obtain an "energy ratio" three times the allowed value of 1, it is necessary to create nine times the earth-wave amplitude (assuming no change in frequency). By referring to Table 11, we can see what this involves in quantity of explosive at different distances. At 1000 ft, for example, to increase ninefold the amplitude produced by 100 lb of explosive would require 2700 lb. Here, then, an allowable "energy ratio" of 1 has a safety factor of 27.

There is now a compelling accumulation of experience to show that rock can be blasted effectively without delivering an "energy ratio" of 1 by elastic waves to nearby structures. This specification of elastic waves is important, because no rules for safety from damage within the plastic zone of a potential crater area have yet been established. Actually, in routine commercial blasting it would be extremely difficult and very wasteful in explosives costs even deliberately to attempt to generate waves carrying an "energy ratio" greater than 1 into the elastic zone. Efficient blasting procedures automatically minimize vibrations in surrounding ground. For this reason, vibration measurements have been used effectively to assess the efficiency of rock blasting, as well as to monitor the vibrations' capacity for damaging property.

Index